BOOKS UNBOUND

MICHAEL JACOBS

NORTH LIGHT BOOKS
CINCINNATI, OHIO
www.artistsnetwork.com

Dedication   *To Judy Pilon Jacobs—you make my heart sing!!*

10 09 08 07 06   5 4 3 2 1

Distributed in Canada by Fraser Direct
100 Armstrong Avenue
Georgetown, ON, Canada L7G 5S4
Tel: (905) 877-4411

Distributed in the U.K. and Europe by David & Charles
Brunel House, Newton Abbot, Devon, TQ12 4PU, England
Tel: (+44) 1626 323200, Fax: (+44) 1626 323319
Email: mail@davidandcharles.co.uk

Distributed in Australia by Capricorn Link
P.O. Box 704, S. Windsor, NSW 2756 Australia
Tel: (02) 4577-3555

Library of Congress Cataloging-in-Publication Data
Jacobs, Michael
    Books unbound / Michael Jacobs.-- 1st ed.
        p. cm.
    Includes index.
    ISBN 1-58180-718-X (alk. paper)
    1. Book design--Handbooks, manuals, etc. 2. Handicraft. I.
Title.
    Z116.A3.J34 2006
    686--dc22
                        2005015488

METRIC CONVERSION CHART

To convert	to	multiply by
Inches	Centimeters	2.54
Centimeters	Inches	0.4
Feet	Centimeters	30.5
Centimeters	Feet	0.03
Yards	Meters	0.9
Meters	Yards	1.1
Sq. Inches	Sq. Centimeters	6.45
Sq. Centimeters	Sq. Inches	0.16
Sq. Feet	Sq. Meters	0.09
Sq. Meters	Sq. Feet	10.8
Sq. Yards	Sq. Meters	0.8
Sq. Meters	Sq. Yards	1.2
Pounds	Kilograms	0.45
Kilograms	Pounds	2.2
Ounces	Grams	28.3
Grams	Ounces	0.035

EDITOR: Jennifer Fellinger
COVER DESIGNERS: Lisa Buchanan and Brian Roeth
INTERIOR DESIGNER: Brian Roeth
LAYOUT ARTIST: Kathy Gardner
PRODUCTION COORDINATOR: Robin Richie
PHOTOGRAPHER: Christine Polomsky and Tim Grondin
PHOTOGRAPHY STYLIST: Jan Nickum

F+W PUBLICATIONS, INC.

ABOUT THE AUTHOR

Michael Jacobs is a designer and teacher who has worked as an artist/craftsman for more than thirty years. His mixed-media sculptures and book works have been exhibited in galleries throughout the United States since 1973 and have appeared in many books and periodicals. Michael, who has taught papercraft and book arts workshops throughout the United States and Canada, is the author of *Cards That Pop Up, Flip & Slide* and co-author of *Creative Correspondence,* both published by North Light Books. Find out more at www.thecreativezone.com.

ACKNOWLEDGMENTS

Special thanks to:

Jennifer Fellinger, editor, for her sense of humor, sensible suggestions for changes, and remarkable ability to condense and organize my step-by-step instructions and manuscript into a tight, flowing book.

Christine Polomsky, photographer, whose good nature makes hanging out in a dark photo studio for a week (almost) enjoyable!

Brian Roeth, designer, who worked with hundreds of photos and lots of text to create a visually exciting and engaging book.

Students, friends and family—your support and encouragement over many years are gratefully accepted and appreciated.

Michael Jacobs, 2006

WHAT IS A BOOK? ...25

UNRAVELING THE BOOK

> > THE ROOTS FOR *BOOKS UNBOUND* go back to 1990, when I designed and built The Kodak Goodwill Games World's Largest Photo Album. This massive book was a mixed-media creation, made from plywood, paper, cardboard, steel, sheet iron, screws, bolts, hot glue, foam padding, waterproof tenting canvas and acrylic paint. The album measured 40" (101.6cm) wide by 27" (68.6cm) high by 8½" (21.6cm) thick, weighed 228 pounds (103kg) and contained 7,254 photos of the Northwest. The album, which was publicly displayed at several locations during the Seattle Goodwill Games, was seen by people from all over the world.

Building this book had a profound effect on me. While figuring out how to bind 184 very large and very heavy pages, I began to view books in a completely new way. Each of the prefabricated components—front and back covers, spine and book block—was

three-dimensional, yet none had much *raison d'être* except as a part of the whole book. For the first time, I looked at books as sculptures, composed of separate parts. This exciting discovery was the impetus behind my decision to construct sculptural books as my personal artistic expression, although subsequent books have been much smaller!

With *Books Unbound*, my goal is to provide fun projects that will challenge your concept of what a "book" is all about. If you are new to bookmaking, practice the basic techniques first, then start with the simpler projects in the first section, "Thinking Outside the Book" (pages 27-77). I have included variations of each project to stimulate you to combine and alter these projects. Mostly, though, I hope *Books Unbound* inspires you to design and construct your own unique book works!

TOOLS AND MATERIALS

> > WHEN I WAS FOUR YEARS OLD, my father made me a very cool toolbox and filled it with a set of basic woodworking tools, which he taught me to use and love. Over the years, that basic kit has changed, but the care and respect for the tools that my father instilled in me remains. Assemble the Basic Tool Kit, and you will be well-equipped to construct most of the projects in this book. A few of the projects also require tools and materials from the Auxiliary Tool Kit, described on the next page.

Basic Tool Kit

The tools are listed in the order they appear in the photo at right, starting at the upper left corner and going clockwise.

Glues and Adhesives I recommend medium or large acid-free, water-soluble glue sticks (I prefer UHU) for smaller projects, and PVA (polyvinyl acetate) applied with a brush for larger projects. Craft glue in a squeeze bottle is excellent for adhering three-dimensional objects.

Needles and Threads A blunt sewing needle and waxed linen, carpet or other strong threads are suggested for the projects in this book. You can take the sharp point off any needle with a fine-tooth file or fine-grit sandpaper.

Self-Healing Cutting Mat These cutting mats are available in a wide range of sizes and are gentle on your knife blades. They last indefinitely.

Stapler An ordinary stapler is used to bind two of the projects in this book.

Rulers For measuring, buy a plastic three-sided architectural ruler with a $1/16$" (2mm) scale (inches divided into sixteenths). All the projects in this book use this scale. For cutting, buy a 12" (30.5cm) steel ruler with cork backing.

Hole Punches Punches are available for creating round, square, diamond, oval, slotted and other decorative shaped holes. A Japanese screw punch allows you to "drill" holes anywhere on paper and board.

BASIC TOOL KIT
Descriptions of the tools (clockwise from the top left corner) are provided on pages 8–9.

Templates *(pictured at center right)* **and French Curves** *(pictured at lower left)* Plastic templates and French curves come in a dizzying array of sizes and shapes. They are invaluable for creating patterns, circles and ovals for windows and curves for customized flaps.

Erasers White vinyl erasers remove pencil marks and lines cleanly, with minimal particle buildup. A clickable eraser in a pen-like holder is one of my favorite tools.

Pencil I highly recommend a mechanical pencil with 0.5mm 2H lead. The hard, narrow lead increases accuracy with thin, non-smearing lines.

Circle Cutters *(pictured at center)* Adjustable circle cutters quickly and accurately cut circles in paper and cardstock.

Knives *(pictured at lower center)* **and Scissors** *(pictured at center left)* Craft knives are excellent tools for cutting straight lines in paper and cardstock. Larger utility knives with heavy-duty blades work best for cutting matboard. Make sure your blade is sharp, as dull blades require greater pressure and are more likely to cause accidents. Scissors are useful for cutting curves.

Awl I recommend an awl with a narrow shaft that is the same diameter throughout its length. The aluminum handled "needle tool" (used by potters) is inexpensive, well-made and easy to manipulate.

Bone Folder and Homemade Scoring Tool Bone folders are used for scoring, creasing and burnishing cardstock and paper. To learn how to fine-tune your bone folder and make a professional scoring tool, see page 13.

Auxiliary Tool Kit

The tools are listed in the order they appear in the photo below, starting at the upper left corner and going clockwise.

Acrylic Paints and Inks Water-soluble acrylic paints and inks are waterproof when they dry, easy to clean up and virtually odorless.

Acrylic Mediums and Glazes Matte, satin and gloss mediums are excellent adhesives for collage papers and can be used as protective finishes on collaged or painted surfaces. They are easy to apply with a paintbrush and easy to clean up with water.

Hammer and Steel Block Use a hammer and steel block (or anvil) to harden and add texture to wire.

Weights Weights come in handy when gluing parts of structures together. I purchased the barbell weight shown in the photo at a thrift shop. A brick or heavy book will work just fine, too.

Goggles Always wear goggles to protect your eyes when working with wire.

Markers I use metallic and indelible markers to "paint" the edges of matboard and to "dye" skewers and other small wooden components.

Threads, Ribbons and Findings These add color and texture to your projects.

Eyelets and Brads *(pictured at center)* Eyelets and brads are available in a variety of shapes, colors and sizes. Use them to attach panels, text blocks and other materials to paper and matboard.

Decorative Scissors and Cutters Use these tools to add custom edges to paper projects.

Pliers Use round-nose pliers *(bottom)* to make loops and coils, flat-nose pliers *(center)* to make right angle bends and to grip and hold wire while working, and end cutters *(top)* to make flush cuts.

Rubber Stamps and Ink Pads Rubber stamps are tailor-made for use with the projects in this book. The number of alphabet, word, image and phrase stamps currently available is mind-boggling.

Paintbrushes A few watercolor brushes in different sizes will come in handy for painting feet and legs for various projects.

Wire Wire is a major component of the last three projects in this book. It is available in a variety of gauges and colors.

AUXILIARY TOOL KIT
Descriptions for the tools and materials (clockwise from the top left corner) are provided above.

TECHNIQUES

> > THE PROJECTS IN THIS BOOK use surprisingly few techniques over and over—techniques that are easy to master! This section teaches you the basics: how to determine grain direction; how to measure, cut and score with precision; how to sew sections to covers; and how to cover boards professionally. You'll also learn how to make sleeves, boxes, button ties and accordion folds.

Determining Grain Direction

Machine-made paper, cardstock and matboard all have a grain direction. This simply means that the fibers from which the paper is made lie primarily in one direction. Why is this important? Because paper folded against the grain— across the direction of the fibers—is weaker, tends to crack and will not lie as flat.

The main folds on book projects will look better and last longer if they are parallel to the grain, so check the materials list to determine whether your project components should be *grain short*, with the grain running parallel to the short dimension of the paper or board, or *grain long*, with the grain running parallel to the long dimension. When

grain direction is specified, this indicates the direction the grain runs after you've cut out your project papers, cardstock or matboard. When working with a square, where the dimensions are the same on all sides, the instructions will specify *grain vertical* or *grain horizontal* to tell you how to orient your square when you make the project.

The label on a ream of $8\frac{1}{2}$" × 11" (21.6cm × 27.9cm) paper or cardstock usually indicates grain direction. If the *11* is underlined, all sheets are grain long. If the *8½* is underlined, the sheets are grain short.

The following photos show two simple and foolproof methods for determining grain direction: *the flex test* and *the spray test*.

The Flex Test

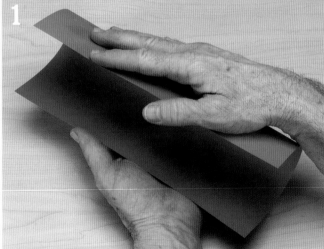

1 BOUNCE PRESS ALONG LENGTH
Bend an $8\frac{1}{2}$" × 11" (21.6cm × 27.9cm) cardstock sheet along its length. "Bounce" the paper up and down along the bend, and sense its resistance to being folded.

2 BOUNCE PRESS ACROSS WIDTH
Now bend the sheet in half across the width and again "bounce" the cardstock up and down. Cardstock always bends with less resistance when folded parallel to the grain. The cardstock above is *grain short*, so it offers less resistance when folded across the width.

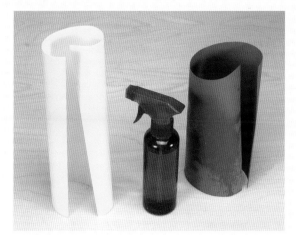

SPRAY PAPER WITH WATER

A simple and dramatic way to determine grain direction is to lightly mist a sheet of cardstock with water. The cardstock will instantly start to curl around the direction of the grain. Imagine grain direction as a tree trunk standing upright inside the curled paper. The yellow sheet in this photo is grain long, and the green sheet is grain short.

Using a Ruler

Rulers are simple tools and easy to master. Practice the techniques below to measure, cut and score accurately. Besides improving the look of your projects, you may even notice a significant reduction in the time needed to complete those projects!

NOT ALL RULERS MEASURE UP

Not only do the two 12" (30.5cm) rulers in this photo vary in length, the distance between the 1" (2.5cm) increments is not consistent! Before buying a ruler, transfer all the inch marks to a piece of paper. Turn the ruler around 180 degrees and line up the 12" mark with the first pencil mark. All the 1" marks should line up precisely. If they do not, the ruler is useless! Always use the same ruler throughout the construction of a project to minimize measuring discrepancies.

ALIGN RULER PROPERLY

When measuring, place the zero point on the ruler on the left edge of the paper, with the ruler parallel to the top and bottom edges. In this photo, the zero point on the top ruler is right at the end of the ruler, and the zero points on the bottom two rulers are set in from the end. Triangular architectural rulers (shown in the middle) have thin lines that rest on the surface of the paper, making it easy to accurately transfer measurements to the paper.

DRAW, SCORE AND CUT PROPERLY

To draw, score or cut lines, first align your ruler properly near the top of the paper. Measure over from the left edge and make tick marks to indicate any lines. Use the same ruler to make tick marks at the bottom of the paper. The metal ruler in the photo has been tilted up to simulate an architectural ruler for greater accuracy.

Scoring, Folding and Creasing

There are two types of folds: *valley folds*, which are made by scoring the front (top) of the cardstock, and *mountain folds*, which are made by scoring the back (bottom) of the cardstock. The following steps demonstrate how to achieve crisp, accurate folds by making valley and mountain scores. To learn more about scoring tools, see page 13.

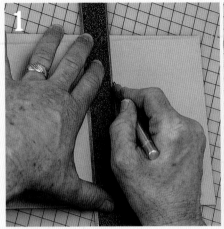

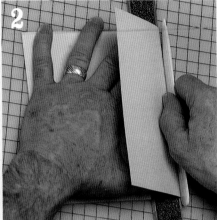

2 BEND CARDSTOCK AT SCORE

Slide your bone folder under the cardstock and run it along the edge of the ruler. The cardstock will bend easily along the score to start a crisp, precise fold.

1 MAKE VALLEY SCORES

Make tick marks at the top and bottom of the cardstock to indicate each valley score. Split the bottom mark with the tip of your scoring tool and slide the lower end of your ruler firmly against the tool, cork side up. Slide the upper end of the ruler to the top mark, then back off just a hair to account for half the thickness of your scoring tool. Run the scoring tool back and forth two or three times against the edge of the ruler to compress the fibers.

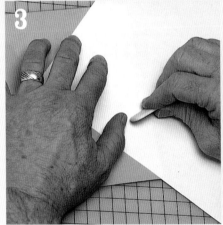

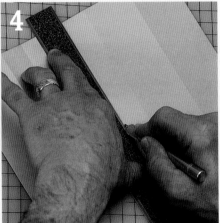

3 CREASE WITH BONE FOLDER

Remove the ruler, fold the cardstock all the way over at the score, and line up the top and bottom edges. Place scrap paper over the fold, and crease with your bone folder. The scrap paper will prevent the bone folder from leaving shiny marks on the cardstock.

4 MAKE MOUNTAIN SCORES

To create accurate mountain folds, make all mountain and valley score tick marks on the valley fold side of the cardstock, about $1/4$" (6mm) from the top and bottom edges. Score and crease all valley folds (see steps 1–3 above). Then, use an awl to pierce holes through all mountain fold tick marks. Turn the cardstock over, line your ruler up with the pierced holes, and score and crease all mountain folds.

TIP

When drawing or scoring a line, placing your ruler corkside up prevents tools from wandering under the edge. I cut cardstock with the ruler corkside up for the same reason. However, I always cut matboard with the ruler corkside down to provide a higher wall for my knife and to keep the ruler from slipping.

Scoring Tools

Bone folders are traditional tools used for scoring, creasing and burnishing. They are handmade and vary in length, width and thickness. Follow the tips at right to shape your bone folder for accurate, crisp scores and folds and to make your own scoring tool.

FINE-TUNE YOUR BONE FOLDER

First, run both long sides back and forth along 100-grit sandpaper to make them straight. Then, hold the bone folder at an angle and round off the edges. Sand the tip to make a slightly rounded point. Smooth the edges and both surfaces with 150-, 200- and 400-grit sandpaper and '"polish" with 600-grit sandpaper. Ultimately, you want the scoring tip to be the same thickness as a jumbo paper clip. Soak the bone folder in mineral oil for several days, turning it periodically. Rinse with hot, soapy water and dry before using.

MAKE YOUR OWN SCORING TOOL

Open a jumbo paper clip and snip off the smaller rounded end with wire cutters, about ¾" (19mm) in length. Lightly hammer the cut ends to flatten. Use pliers to insert the ends into the open chuck of a medium craft knife handle and tighten firmly. This lifetime tool is ideal for scoring cardstock and heavy text paper.

Covering a Board with 90 Degree Corners

Covering and lining boards is a basic technique necessary for many of the projects in this book. The step-by-step instructions below are easy to master, and they produce professional results every time.

1 ROUND EDGES OF BOARD
Run the blunt end of the bone folder at a 45 degree angle along the edges on both sides of the board three or four times, applying firm pressure. This process compresses the fibers along the edges of the board and rounds them slightly, making the board easier to cover.

2 ADHERE BOARD TO COVER PAPER
Run a glue stick or brush PVA over one surface of the board and center it on the cover paper with the grain on each component running parallel. Use the bone folder to lightly adhere the board to the paper, as shown here, then flip the board over and burnish the cover paper to the board, working outward from the center.

3 CLIP CORNERS AND CURL
Cut off the corners of the cover paper about ⅛" (3mm) from the corners of the board. You will be left with four "turn-ins." Curve all four turn-ins around the board by sliding each edge of the board against a clean, smooth surface in a semicircular motion. This makes it easier to glue down the turn-ins.

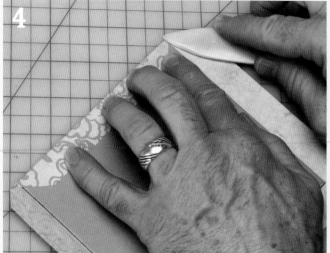

4 GLUE AND TUCK TURN-INS

Run a glue stick or brush PVA over one turn-in, fold it over, and burnish the turn-in to the board. Use the tip of your bone folder to tuck both paper corners around the ends of the board. Repeat with the turn-in on the opposite side. Then glue down and burnish the two remaining turn-ins.

5 ADHERE LINER

Run a glue stick or brush PVA over the inside surface of the liner and attach it to the uncovered portion of the board, centered on all sides, with the grain on the board and liner running parallel. Burnish the liner to the board, working outward from the center.

Covering a Board with Truncated Corners

Two of the projects in this book are made with boards that have truncated corners. Covering these boards is simple, and the "missing corners" add a sophisticated look to many book structures.

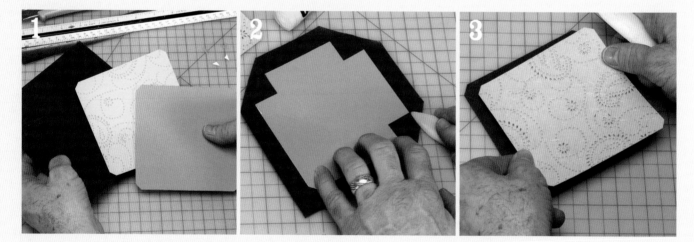

1 PREPARE COMPONENTS

Cut matboard, cover paper and liner paper to the desired size. Make pencil marks on each edge of the matboard 1/4" (6mm) from the corners. Line up the ruler on the marks and cut corners off. Run the blunt end of the bone folder at a 45 degree angle along the edges and corners on both sides of the board.

2 GLUE CORNERS

Follow step 2 on page 13 and attach the board to the cover paper. Run a glue stick or brush PVA over one cover paper corner and fold it over the cut corner of the board. Burnish the corner to the board and tuck each side of the corner around the sides of the board. Repeat process with the three remaining corners. You will be left with four turn-ins.

3 GLUE LINER

Curve all four turn-ins around the board as you did in step 3 on page 13. Glue and burnish each turn-in to the inside of the board, then run the bone folder firmly over each corner to compress the layers of the cover paper and reduce bulk. Glue the liner to the uncovered board, as shown, and burnish in place, working outward from the center.

Making a Basic Pamphlet Stitch

In 1971, when I owned a custom leather shop, I decided to purchase a used sewing machine—an industrial Singer 111W—from a shoe repair man, who demonstrated the machine by sewing down the middle of a wooden yardstick! I bought that machine and have been sewing ever since. Today, however, my sewing is done by hand to attach sections to covers with a pamphlet stitch.

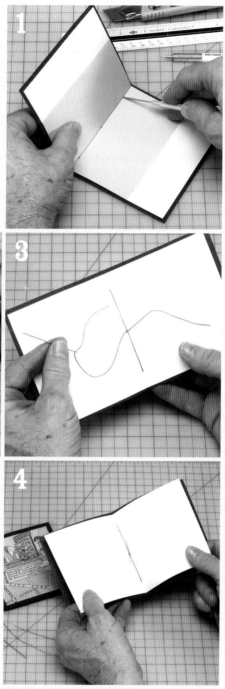

1 PIERCE COVER AND PAGES

Make a cardstock sewing station template the same height as the pages, with three dots on the scored center fold to indicate *sewing stations* (see *Definition*, below). Place the *section* (see *Definition*, below) and the template in the fold inside the cover, centered top to bottom. Pierce holes with an awl through top sewing station 1, center station 2 and bottom station 3. Remove the sewing station template.

3 FINISH SEWING

Run the needle out through station 3 to the back side of the cover and pull gently to remove slack. Then, run the needle to the inside through station 2, with the needle end of the thread and the tail end of the thread on opposite sides of the center section of the thread. Remove needle.

2 BEGIN SEWING

Cut thread about three times the length of the spine. Pull approximately 2" (5.1cm) of the thread through the eye of a needle. Starting from the inside, run the needle out through center station 2 and back to the inside through station 1. Pinch the tail to prevent the thread from pulling through station 2, and pull gently to remove slack.

4 TIE KNOT

Tie thread ends in a square knot around the center section of the thread and trim the ends to approximately ¾" (19mm). Artist Lynne Kelly taught me this Girl Scout rhyme for tying a square knot: "Right over left and left over right, makes a square knot good and tight."

NOTE: *If you start sewing from the inside, as I did, your knot and thread ends will be on the inside. If you start on the outside, your knot and thread ends will be on the outside, ready to attach beads, findings, etc.*

DEFINITION

A *sheet* is a single piece of paper with a front and a back side. When you fold a sheet in half, you create a *folio* with four pages, and the fold creates a hinge. Two or more folios nested inside each other create a *section*. Sections are sewn to covers at the hinge fold through pierced holes called *sewing stations*.

Making a Five-Station Stitch

The five-station stitch is recommended when sewing taller sections to covers. It is stronger than the three-station pamphlet stitch, and the additional stations pull the folios closer together at the section fold, preventing any unsightly gaps.

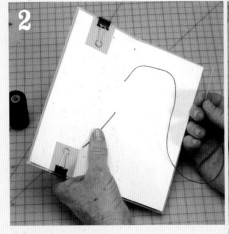

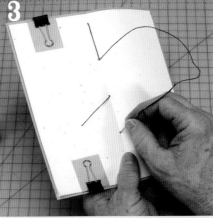

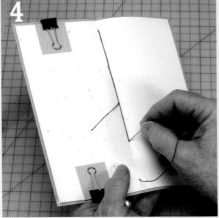

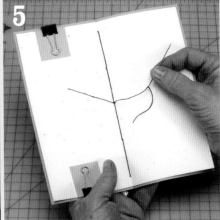

1 PIERCE HOLES IN COVER AND PAGES

Make five dots on the center fold of the section where you want your holes to be. (NOTE: *This is an alternative to making a sewing station template.*) Center the section inside the cover and pierce holes through the dots; the top hole is 1, the second hole is 2, the third hole is 3, and so on.

2 BEGIN SEWING

Clip the section to the cover if desired. Cut thread four times the length of the spine. Pull approximately 2" (5.1cm) of the thread through the eye of a needle. Starting from the inside, run the needle through center station 3 and back to the inside through station 2. Pinch the tail and pull gently to remove slack.

3 CONTINUE SEWING

Run the needle out through station 1 and back to the inside through station 2, then out through station 4. Pull gently to remove slack.

4 CONTINUE SEWING

Run the needle from the back through station 5 to the inside, and out through station 4. Pull gently to remove slack.

5 FINISH SEWING

Run the needle in through center station 3 and tie a square knot around the center section of thread (see step 4 on page 15). Trim the ends of the thread to ³⁄₄" (19mm) in length.

Making a Sleeve

When I make custom-fitted *sleeves* for book projects, I use *paper rulers* (see *Definitions*, at right). They are much more accurate than steel or architectural rulers, and they are easier to use! Learn how to make the sleeve below using a paper ruler, then construct boxes, covers, slipcases and more with this simple and elegant tool.

1 MARK RULER FOR HEIGHT OF SLEEVE

Position the book horizontally on your work surface, and place the edge of a narrow strip of paper along the spine. Make a pencil mark on this "paper ruler" at the desired height for the sleeve, as shown.

2 MARK SLEEVE CARDSTOCK

Place the sleeve cardstock facedown in a horizontal position. Place the left end of the paper ruler flush with the left end of the cardstock. Transfer the pencil mark to the top edge of the cardstock. Slide the paper ruler to the bottom edge of the cardstock, and again transfer the mark to the cardstock, as shown.

3 CUT OUT SLEEVE COMPONENT

Remove the paper ruler. Line up a metal ruler on the marks and cut the sleeve component away from the right-hand section of the cardstock.

4 MARK RULER FOR WIDTH OF BOOK

Turn the paper ruler over and place the book in the upper left corner, with the spine flush with the left edge of the paper ruler. Make a pencil mark at the top edge of the paper ruler, just a hair to the right of the foredge of the book.

5 MARK RULER FOR DEPTH OF BOOK

Stand the book on its spine and place the left edge of the spine on the pencil mark. Make another pencil mark just a hair out from the right side of the spine.
NOTE: *In this photo, my paper ruler has been turned around for purposes of clarity.*

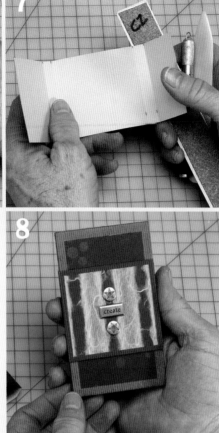

7 SCORE SLEEVE

Remove the paper ruler and valley score, fold and crease the four vertical lines indicated by the pencil marks, as shown. Fold the left portion of the sleeve to the right at the second valley fold. Glue up the inside surface of the small *glue flap* (see *Definition*, below) at right, fold it over, and burnish it to the top of the left portion.

8 DECORATE SLEEVE

A custom-fitted sleeve made with a paper ruler slides on easily, yet has the correct amount of friction to stay in place. I lined my sleeve with decorative paper and added three eyelets to "create" a focal point.

6 MARK SLEEVE

With the sleeve facedown in a horizontal position, line up the left edges of the sleeve and the paper ruler. Transfer the marks on the ruler to the top edge of the sleeve. Slide the left edge of the ruler to the second pencil mark on the sleeve and again transfer the marks on the ruler to the sleeve. Mark up the bottom edge of the sleeve in the same way, as shown.

DEFINITION

GLUE FLAP: A glue flap or glue strip is a section of paper or cardstock protruding from the top, side or bottom of a component, defining a specific area to be coated with glue.

Making an Open-Top Box

The simple box below is a sleeve with a built-in bottom. After you construct this box using a paper ruler, you will realize the size relationships of the various parts of a box. You will then be able to use paper rulers to construct accurate boxes in any size.

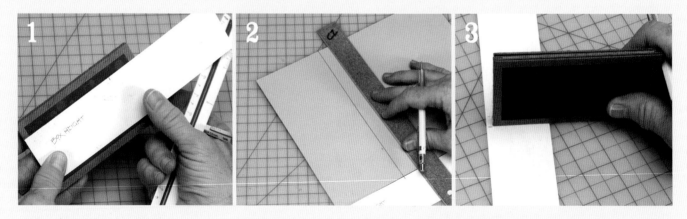

1 MARK RULER FOR BOX HEIGHT

Place the book flat on your work surface in a horizontal position. Make a pencil mark on the top edge of the paper ruler to indicate the height of the box.

2 TRANSFER MARK TO CARDSTOCK

Place the box cardstock facedown in a horizontal position. Transfer the mark on the ruler to the top and bottom edges of the cardstock. Line up the ruler with the pencil marks and draw a vertical line on the cardstock.

3 MARK RULER FOR SPINE DEPTH

Turn the paper ruler over and place it in a vertical position. With the book flat, place the spine flush with the bottom edge of the ruler, and make a pencil mark on the ruler, just a hair out from the foredge. Stand the book on its spine, and place the front edge of the spine on the pencil mark. Make another pencil mark just a hair out from the back edge of the spine.

4 TRANSFER MARKS TO CARDSTOCK

Position the box cardstock vertically with the pencil line at the top. Place the left edge of the ruler flush with the left edge of the cardstock and transfer the pencil marks to the top edge of the cardstock. Slide the ruler to the right with the left edge of the ruler on the second pencil mark, and again transfer the pencil marks on the paper ruler to the cardstock, as shown. Then, slide the paper ruler to the bottom of the box cardstock and mark up the bottom edge in the same way.

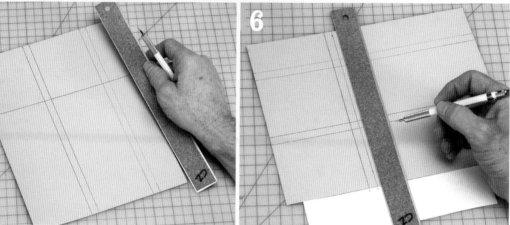

5 DRAW VERTICAL LINES ON CARDSTOCK

Line up the metal ruler with the pencil marks at the top and bottom of the box cardstock and draw four vertical lines, as shown.

6 DRAW ONE MORE LINE ON CARDSTOCK

Turn the paper 90 degrees, positioning the box cardstock horizontally with the narrow section at the top. Place the left pencil mark on the paper ruler on the vertical line and transfer the right mark to the top and bottom edges of the box cardstock. Line up the ruler on the pencil marks and draw a vertical line, as shown.

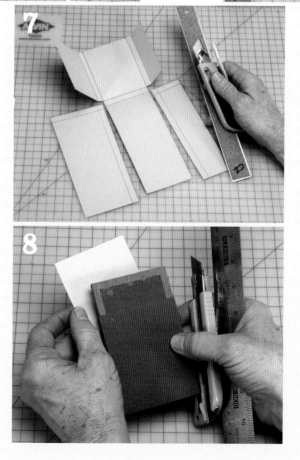

7 SCORE LINES

Cut out the bottom left and bottom right sections. Valley score, fold and crease all remaining lines.

8 FINISH BOX

Fold the left section of the box to the right, and the smaller right section to the left. Then, fold the long bottom section up and turn the box over left to right. Cut off the top section flush with the top edge of the back of the box. Glue the three back panels together and burnish with the bone folder.

Adding a Flap to Your Box

I made these three short boxes and the two sleeves with the same paper ruler. Look closely and you will see that the third box also has a top flap tucked under the sleeve. It's as easy as 1-2-3 to add flaps to open top boxes. First, place your flap cardstock vertically, facedown. Transfer the two marks denoting the spine width measurement on your paper ruler to the center of the flap cardstock at the left and right edges. Second, line up the ruler with the marks, and valley score, fold and crease the two lines. Third, glue up the inside bottom section and attach and burnish the flap to the back of the box, as shown at right in the photo.

Large Cardstock Box

The box below is just the right size for the Book in a Box on page 84. The width of the two outside vertical sections determines the height of the box. The top horizontal section becomes the flap, while the second and fourth sections are the top and bottom of the box and determine its length and width. The third and fifth sections are the front and back of the box. When you assemble the box, observe the relationships of these sections. Then use a paper ruler and construct a similar box. By then, your mantra will be: *Paper rules!*

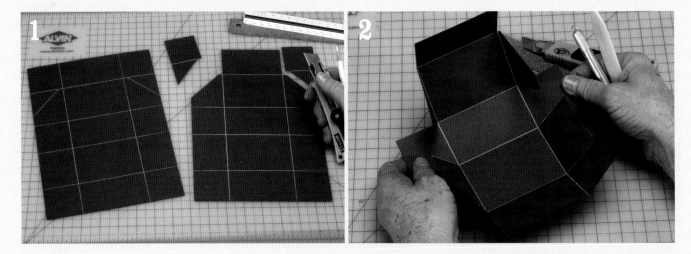

1 PREPARE BOX CARDSTOCK

Place the box cardstock facedown in a vertical position. Draw vertical lines 2" (5.1cm) and 5¾" (14.6cm) from the left edge. Then, draw horizontal lines 2" (5.1cm), 4½" (11.4cm), 6½" (16.5cm) and 9" (22.9cm) from the top edge. Make dots on the left and right edges 3¾" (9.5cm) from the top, and on the top horizontal line 1¾" (4.4cm) in from the left and right edges. Connect the dots and cut away the upper portions of the cardstock, as shown at right.

2 SCORE AND CUT CARDSTOCK

Valley score, fold and crease the two vertical lines. Open the sides and cut the bottom three horizontal lines from the vertical scores out through the left and right edges of the cardstock. Valley score, fold and crease the four horizontal lines.

3 GLUE FLAPS TO BOX SIDES

Place the box cardstock facedown, as shown. Fold the bottom left side flap to the center panel and run a glue stick over the flap. Attach the flap to the left side of the box and burnish with a bone folder. Repeat with the bottom right side flap.

4 GLUE OTHER FLAPS TO BOX SIDES

Run a glue stick over the outside surface of the two remaining square side flaps and attach them to the inside surface of the box sides, over the flaps from step 1. Burnish with a bone folder.

5 FINISH BOX

Shape the front panel and decorate the box as desired. Side panels tuck inside the box, and the front panel can tuck inside or be held closed with a sleeve around the entire box.

Making an Accordion-Fold Insert

When I first started making accordion-fold pages, the folds rarely lined up to my satisfaction when I was finished. I finally learned the following technique, which is an easy way to make accurate accordion-fold inserts. Start with a piece of text paper (grain short) and cut it to the desired width, with the length equal to eight times the height of one accordion page.

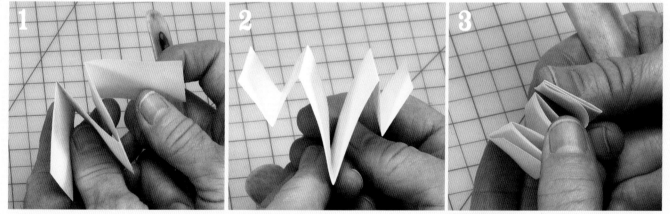

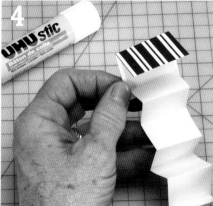

1 MAKE FIRST FOLDS

Fold your paper strip in half and crease the fold. Fold each end back to the center fold and crease each fold.

2 CONTINUE FOLDING

Fold each end to the folds made in step 1 and crease the folds, as shown.

3 FINISH FOLDING

Open the structure flat, then reverse the center fold. Fold the bottom section to the middle fold and crease. Turn the partially completed accordion-fold unit over and fold the bottom section on that side to the center fold and crease.

4 ATTACH INSERT TO COVER

Glue up the outside surface of page 1 and attach it to the inside of the cover, centered on all sides. Burnish.

Making Triangular Accordion-Fold Books

Follow these simple steps to make an accordion-fold book with equilateral triangle covers. The width and length of your page insert paper will vary, depending on the size of your triangle covers and the desired number of pages.

The steps below describe the process for constructing a triangular accordion-fold book to fit inside the Three-Sided Triangle Book on pages 94–97. To construct larger or smaller triangular accordion-fold books, first create two equilateral triangle covers to the desired size. Cut the page paper ³⁄₄" (19mm) narrower in width than the length of the sides of your covers; to determine the length of the page paper, multiply the width by the number of pages desired.

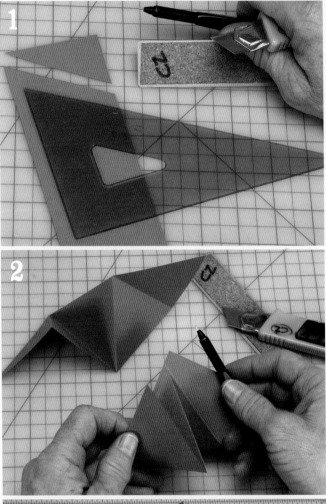

1 PREPARE PAGE PAPERS
Cut two text-weight page papers 2 ³⁄₄" × 10" (7.0cm × 25.4cm), grain short. Trace a 60 degree angle to the top of each page paper. Cut along the pencil lines and set the top sections aside.

2 ACCORDION-FOLD PAGE PAPERS
Accordion-fold each page paper back and forth using the 60 degree angle as a guide to create triangular sections. Cut off any excess paper at the end flush with the last fold.

3 GLUE TOGETHER
Glue two page papers together, as shown, and burnish with a bone folder.

4 ATTACH PAGE INSERT TO COVERS
Trace the book cover pattern on page 99 twice onto a sheet of cardstock, then cut out the covers. Glue up the outer surface of one end of the triangle accordion-fold page insert and attach it to the inside of one equilateral triangle cover. Burnish. Repeat process with second cover. Decorate as desired.

Making a Two-Button Tie

Two-button ties not only hold book covers closed, they also add texture and color and require the reader to interact playfully with the book. Don't stop with two buttons—place three buttons on the front cover and one on the back cover to create beautiful patterns when you wrap them with string.

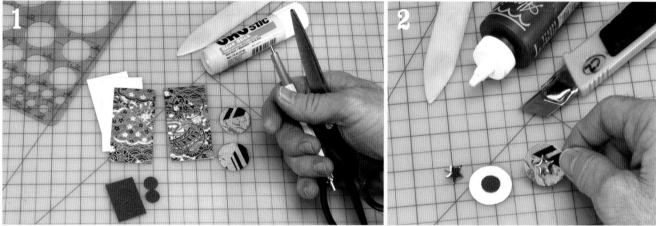

1 PREPARE BUTTONS

Glue two small pieces of cardstock together, line with decorative paper and burnish. Draw two circles (or other desired button shapes) on the decorative paper and cut them out. Glue two small pieces of cardstock together and burnish. Trace and cut out two ½" (13mm) circles from the cardstock to act as spacers.

2 ADD BRADS TO BUTTONS

Place the two buttons facedown. Glue one spacer to the center of each button and burnish. Turn buttons over. Cut a slit in the center of each button, just long enough to accommodate the width of brad prongs. Place one brad through the slit on each button.

3 ATTACH BUTTONS

Cut tiny slits in each side component (here, the left and right panels) and insert brad prongs on the buttons through slits. Bend the prongs over and flatten them with a bone folder. Tie string around one of the buttons, then wrap the string around both buttons.

TIP

For a one-button tie, attach one button as described above. Then, cut a slit where the second button would be. Run the end of a length of thread through the slit. Secure the end in place on the inside surface of the cover with a paper liner.

WHAT IS A BOOK?

> > Ever since childhood, I have liked art and craft objects that incorporate words. Artist books are the ideal medium for my ongoing artistic expression—these books blend design, form, content and craft into a sculptural object that can be read on many levels (no pun intended!).

But what is a book?! The dictionary defines *book* as "a printed work on sheets of paper bound together, usually between two protective covers," and *bookbinding* as "the art, trade or business of binding books." Many of the objects I have designed over the years do not fit the dictionary description of *book*, though they contain text and are bound in various ways. For years I was comfortable with my own definition of *book*: A small, intimate, handheld object that reveals information over time.

I always ask the artists in my sculptural bookmaking workshops the following question: What is minimally required for an object to be called "a book"? Here's one of the many answers that really intrigued me: "In *On Writing*, Stephen King defines writing as a form of telepathy because writing transmits the ideas of the author over time and space to another person (I liked that). To me, books are material conveyances for telepathy—just an extension of King's idea."

I am presently leaning toward the student's take on Stephen King's idea. What is your definition of *book*? As you construct the projects in *Books Unbound*, ask yourself if they are, in fact, books. Then again, I hope these projects cause you to rethink what books are all about. Trust me, they *are* books. I said so!

THINKING OUTSIDE THE BOOK

> > THIS FIRST SECTION OF *BOOKS UNBOUND* CONTAINS eleven book projects combined loosely into three categories—Super Simple Books, Travel Journals and Books With Pockets. They are easy to construct and include many unique features and possibilities. You will learn how to make:

* books requiring very few tools, little measuring, and nothing more elaborate than a glue stick and a stapler to bind the covers and pages together

* book structures with a variety of page inserts and throwouts (parts of pages that unfold and extend beyond the confines of the covers)

* a book with a cover and pages that are interchangeable (think about that for a minute—is this guy nuts, and why did he design such a book?!)

* three compact journals—two with mini portfolios to hold paper mementos from your trips

* two books that take on a whole new attitude when you add feet

These first eleven projects are intended to get you thinking outside the box (or book?). Have fun, enjoy the construction process, and think about ways to change these books. Challenge yourself to make hybrids and to alter and combine two or more structures to create a novel (pun intended!) structure of your own.

FOLD-AND-CUT BOOK

TOOLS AND MATERIALS

basic tool kit (page 8)

COVER
4⅜" × 7¾"
(11.7cm × 19.7cm)
piece of cardstock
(grain short)

PAGES
8½" × 11"
(21.6cm × 27.9cm)
piece of text paper
(grain short)

SLEEVE
2¼" × 7⅛"
(5.7cm × 20.0cm)
piece of cardstock
(grain short)

> > PLAYING AROUND WITH PAPER is a relaxing and wonderful way for me to get the creative juices flowing. The Fold-and-Cut Book "happened" one day when I was playing with sheets of paper, a pencil, a knife and a ruler. I had no agenda and quickly got caught up in the simple act of folding paper. The folds on one sheet evolved over time and led to the creation of this super simple interactive book. Play around with paper and come up with some Fold-and-Cut Books of your own design!

1 CREATE COVER

Place the cover cardstock facedown in a horizontal position. Measuring from the left edge, draw light vertical pencil lines at 1⅝" (4.1cm) and 4¾" (12.1cm). Valley score, fold and crease each line. Erase the pencil lines.

2 FOLD TEXT-WEIGHT PAPER

Place the paper for the pages facedown in a horizontal position. Measuring from the left edge, draw light vertical pencil lines at 5⅜" (13.7cm) and 5⅝" (14.3cm). Fold the top edge of the paper to the bottom edge and crease the fold. Open the fold and smooth out the paper.

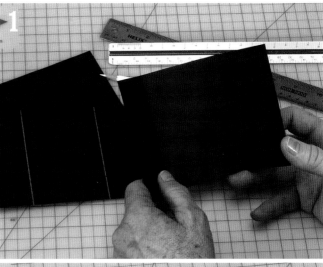

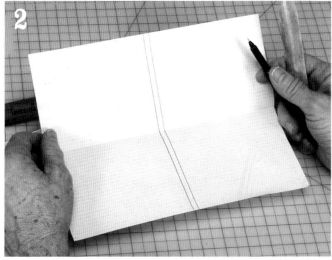

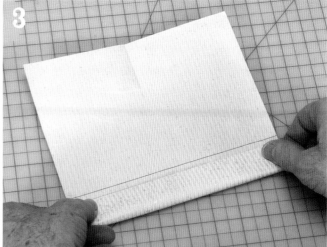

3 FOLD AND CREASE ONE END OF PAPER

With the paper in a vertical position, fold the bottom edge to meet the first horizontal line. Crease the fold. Then, bring the bottom fold to the first line, being careful not to let the bottom edge of the paper slip beyond the first line. Crease the fold.

4 FOLD AND CREASE OTHER END OF PAPER

Turn the unit around so the top edge is at the bottom, running horizontally. Repeat the folding procedure from step 3.

TIP

You can change the size of Fold-and-Cut Book pages by varying the size of the paper you start with, and you can make Fold-and-Cut Books from square paper, too. Glue two books together back to back to hold additional text or to tell separate stories.

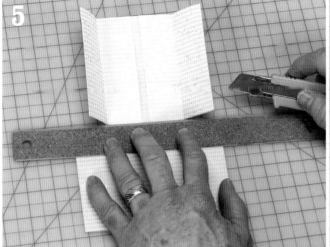
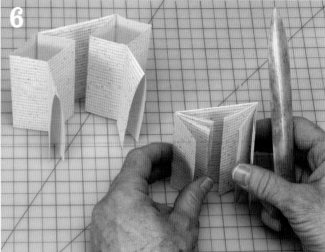

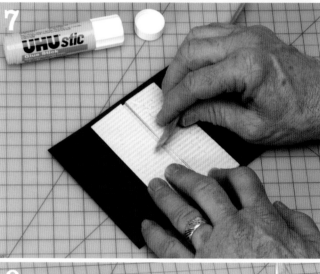

5 CUT ALONG FOLDS

Open the top and bottom folds, then position the unit as shown above. With a knife and ruler (or scissors), cut along the horizontal middle fold from the left folded edge to just beyond the first vertical fold. Make a similar cut from the right folded edge, stopping just past the vertical fold.

6 COMPLETE UNIT

Open the page unit and fold it in half horizontally, then open the two slits at the top, as shown at left. Flatten the unit and fold the sections at the left and right to the center and crease. Pages may be opened individually, and then lifted up at the horizontal fold to expose hidden text on the entire inside surface.

7 ATTACH PAGE UNIT INSIDE COVER

Close the page unit and run a glue stick over the back center section. Attach the unit to the middle inside section of the cover, centering it top to bottom and side to side. (You have the option of placing the horizontal fold of the page unit at the top or bottom.) Burnish the page unit in place.

8 CREATE SLEEVE

Place the sleeve cardstock facedown in a horizontal position. Measuring from the left edge, draw light vertical pencil lines at 1½" (3.8cm) and 4¾" (12.1cm). Valley score, fold and crease each line.

9 FINISH SLEEVE

Fold the sleeve's right section to the left, and the small glue flap to the right. Run a pencil along the edge of the glue flap. Lift the glue flap and run a glue stick over the traced area. Burnish the glue flap to the sleeve.

10 DECORATE AND PLACE BOOK IN SLEEVE

Embellish the front of the sleeve as desired and slide the finished sleeve over the cover to keep the book closed.

NOTE: *In lieu of a sleeve, you can make a one- or two-button tie closure for the Fold-and-Cut Book; for instructions, see page 23.*

ALTERNATE ENDINGS

This Fold-and-Cut Book features French doors that meet at the center. The button on the sleeve was cut from a wine cork and is held in place with a brad.

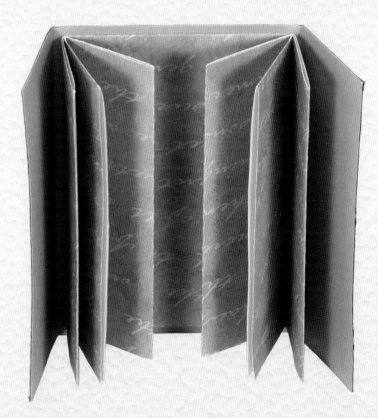

ONE-PIECE COVER BOOK

TOOLS AND MATERIALS

basic tool kit (page 8)

hammer

ONE-PIECE COVER
8½" x 11" (21.6cm × 27.9cm) piece of cardstock (grain short)

PAGES
five 4¼" × 8¼" (10.8cm × 21.0cm) pieces of text paper (grain long)

SPINE WRAP
1½" × 8½" (3.8cm × 21.6cm) piece of plain or decorative text paper (grain long)

> > PLAYING AROUND WITH MOUNTAIN AND VALLEY FOLDS on sheets of cardstock provided the impetus for the One-Piece Cover Book. The cover is made from a sheet of 8½" × 11" (21.6cm × 27.9cm) cardstock, and the pages are bound with staples. Turn-ins at the foredge are folded over for strength and can hold additional loose pages or accordion-fold pages. Adjust the scores and make larger One-Piece Cover Books from 8½" × 14" (21.6cm × 35.6cm) and 11" × 17" (27.9cm × 43.2cm) sheets of cardstock.

1 BEGIN COVER

Place the cover cardstock facedown in a horizontal position. Measuring from the left edge, draw light vertical pencil lines at 1" (2.5cm), 4¾" (12.1cm), 5½" (14.0cm) and 10" (25.4cm). Valley score the 1", 5½" and 10" lines, and mountain score the 4¾" line. Fold and crease all the scores.

2 GLUE AND BURNISH TURN-INS

Using *glue guards* (see *Definition*, below) to protect your work surface, run a glue stick over the inside surface of the 1" (2.5cm) turn-ins. Burnish the turn-ins to the inside of the cover. (These turn-ins strengthen the cover and provide a handsome fold at the foredge.)

3 FORM BOOK BLOCK

Stack the pages and place in a vertical position. Shape and decorate the foredges if desired. Staple the pages together at the center, just in from the left edge. Flatten the staple by lightly hammering it.

4 POSITION BOOK BLOCK IN COVER

Close the cover and fold the top to the left at the mountain fold. Place the stapled edge of the book block snugly against the valley fold, as shown, and center it top to bottom.

DEFINITION

GLUE GUARD: Glue guards are clean scraps of paper used when applying glue to a component to protect the work surface and confine the glue to a specific area on the component.

5 STAPLE SPINE

Close the cover. Staple three times along the spine, about ½" (13mm) in from the center fold. Flatten the staples by lightly hammering them.

6 FINISH BOOK

Fold the spine wrap in half along the length and crease the fold. Run a glue stick over the inside surface, then insert the center fold of the cover into the spine wrap, as shown. Push it snugly into place and burnish both sides. Embellish the cover as desired.

ADD SOME KICK!

Make One-Piece Cover Books from any rectangular or square piece of cardstock, in any size. Substitute accordion-fold pages in place of the loose pages, staple more accordion-fold pages under either or both the foredge turn-ins, and have them open toward the top or bottom. The photos below show more possibilities.

I made a one-piece cover and cut it into two parts. Then, I stapled loose pages to the center of each cover and lined the spines. I stapled pages inside the foredge turn-ins and lined the turn-ins. This is a fast and easy way to make multiple books!

The pages stapled to the foredge turn-ins on the smaller book open to the left and right, respectively, and do not interfere with the center pages.

The larger book features loose pages stapled under the turn-in on the front cover. The turn-in on the back cover was glued down without adding any pages. When the cover is opened, the front page of each book block is completely visible.

Feet, Legs and Risers

Many of the projects in this book are designed to have feet or legs. Glue stick caps, plastic bottle caps, wooden blocks, wooden spheres and cylinders, cardboard tubes, and deodorant sticks and caps are just a few of the many objects that can be painted or collaged and transformed into colorful feet, legs and risers. Look at all small throwaway objects as potential feet! I used a variety of acrylic mediums and glazes to collage and protect the feet, legs and risers shown here.

ALTERNATE ENDINGS

Take the One-Piece Cover Book a step further and turn it into a striking, freestanding sculpture. To do so, simply cover a board, attach four feet, and glue the back of your book to the top surface (see "Feet, Legs and Risers," above)—or display your book by standing it up on a riser, as shown here.

CHECKERBOARD BOOK

TOOLS AND MATERIALS

basic tool kit (page 8)

patterns (page 41)

FRONT AND BACK COVERS
two 4" × 6" (10.2cm × 15.2cm) pieces of cardstock (grain short)

PAGES 1, 3 AND 5
6¼" × 8¼" (15.9cm × 21.0cm) piece of cardstock (grain long)

PAGES 2 AND 4
4¼" × 8½" (10.8cm × 21.6cm) piece of cardstock (grain short)

PAGE 6
3¾" × 5⅞" (9.5cm × 14.9cm) piece of cardstock (grain short)

SPINE WRAP
2¼" × 4" (5.7cm × 10.2cm) piece of thin, decorative paper (grain long)

> > WHEN I TEACH THE CHECKERBOARD BOOK, I am constantly amazed by the innovative ideas students incorporate into this simple book structure. They have used the stair-stepped page corners to cleverly conceal and reveal words, and they have created spectacular interactive books with the addition of colorful head, tail and foredge throwouts. Once you have made a Checkerboard Book following the steps on pages 37–39, play around with the checkerboard concept and take this little book to a whole new level!

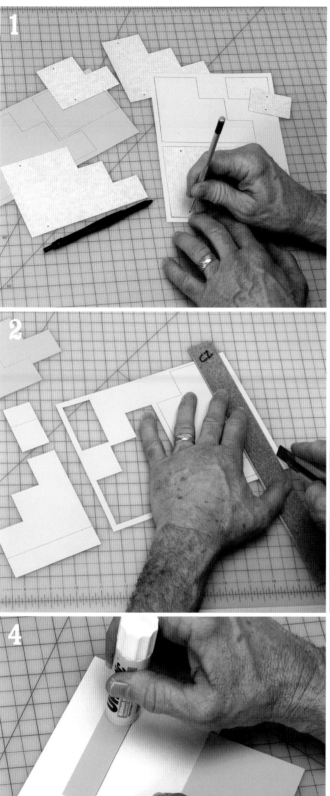

1 TRACE AND PIERCE PATTERNS

Place cardstock for pages faceup on work surface. Trace patterns for pages 1, 3 and 5 and pages 2 and 4 onto the cardstock, as shown. Pierce one hole through each dot on every pattern.

2 PENCIL IN LINES AND CUT OUT PAGES

Line up a ruler with the two pierced holes on each page and draw light vertical pencil lines from top to bottom. The narrow panels to the left of the pencil lines define the glue strips. Cut out pages 1 to 5 using a ruler and knife.

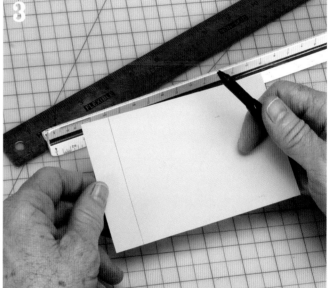

3 PENCIL IN LINE ON PAGE 6

Place the cardstock for page 6 faceup in a horizontal position. Measure $7/8$" (22mm) from the left edge and draw a light vertical pencil line to define the glue strip.

4 APPLY GLUE

Place page 6 on scrap paper with the straight edge of a glue guard along the pencil line, and run the glue stick over the narrow glue strip.

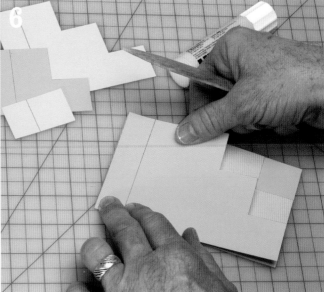

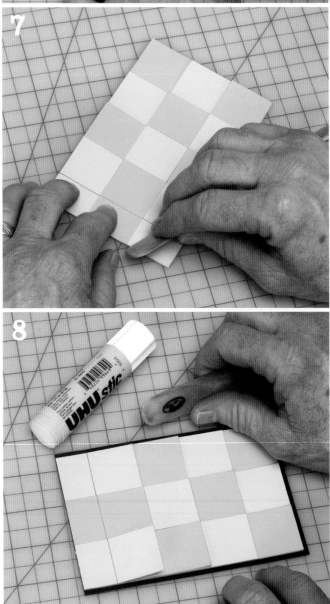

5 GLUE PAGE 5 TO PAGE 6

Remove the glue guard and scrap paper, and position page 5 over page 6. Square up the pages, then burnish.

6 ADD PAGE 4

Place page unit 5–6 on scrap paper and position a fresh glue guard along the vertical line on page 5. Run the glue stick over the glue strip and attach page 4. Burnish.

7 ADD PAGES 3, 2 AND 1

Use scrap papers and fresh glue guards for each remaining page and attach pages 3, 2 and 1 in the same manner as pages 4 and 5, burnishing each page as it is glued in place.

8 ATTACH BACK COVER

Place the back cover cardstock facedown in a horizontal position. Measure $7/8$" (22mm) from the left edge and draw a light vertical pencil line. Using a fresh glue guard, run a glue stick over the glue strip. Attach the book block to the back cover, flush with the left edge (spine) and centered top to bottom. Burnish.

9 PREPARE FRONT COVER

With the front cover faceup in a horizontal position, draw a light vertical pencil line ⁷⁄₈" (22mm) from the left edge (spine). Valley score the line, fold and crease.

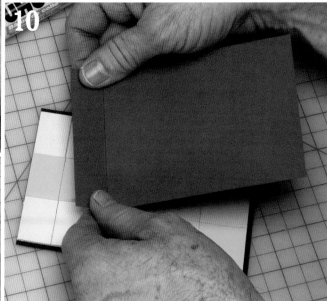

10 ATTACH FRONT COVER

Using a glue guard, run a glue stick over the glue strip on the book block. Remove the guard and attach the inside surface of the front cover to the book block so that it is flush on all sides with the back cover. Burnish the glue strip area. Allow the glue to dry.

11 SCORE EACH PAGE INDIVIDUALLY

Open the front cover. Place the ruler edge along the fold, then valley score page 1. Turn the page and crease fold. Place the ruler edge along the fold on page 1 and score page 2. Crease fold. Score and crease pages 3, 4 and 5, one at a time in a similar manner. This method of scoring places each successive score slightly closer to the foredge of the book and compensates for the page thickness when turning pages.

12 ADD SPINE AND FINISH COVER

Run a glue stick over the inside surface of the spine wrap and attach the leading edge just slightly to the left of the valley fold on the front cover, flush at the top and bottom. Fold the spine wrap tightly around the spine to the back cover and burnish both sides. If desired, embellish front and back covers. Using a circle cutter, I cut out a circle on the front cover to expose the checkerboard pages.

A *throwout* refers to the part of a page that unfolds and extends beyond the book covers. Any page can incorporate a throwout. I constructed each of the three throwouts on the Checkerboard Book at right with the page 4 pattern (page 41). The head throwout, shown at left, is the width of page 4 and twice the height, with the fold at the top. The foredge throwout, shown at right, is the height of page 4 and twice the width, with the fold on the right. The tail throwout is the width of page 4 and twice the height, with the fold at the bottom. I traced the page 4 pattern to these prefolded page papers and cut away the upper right portion to create the throwouts. Then, I removed a 1⅛" (2.9cm) strip from the spine portion of each throwout to keep it out of the binding area and to provide clearance so it opens easily.

ADD SOME KICK!

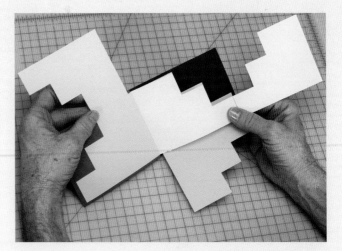

The Checkerboard Book in this photo shows three throwouts, all constructed from the checkerboard page 4 pattern (page 41). The page on the left, scored and creased at the head, unfolds upward; the middle page, scored and creased at the foredge, opens out to the right; and the bottom page, scored and creased at the tail, opens downward.

ALTERNATE ENDINGS

Each page in this Checkerboard Book incorporates a head, foredge or tail throwout. It is fun for the reader to interact with the throwouts to uncover hidden text, and the fully opened pages create a beautiful wall sculpture!

PATTERNS FOR CHECKERBOARD BOOK

Enlarge patterns at 125% to bring to full size.

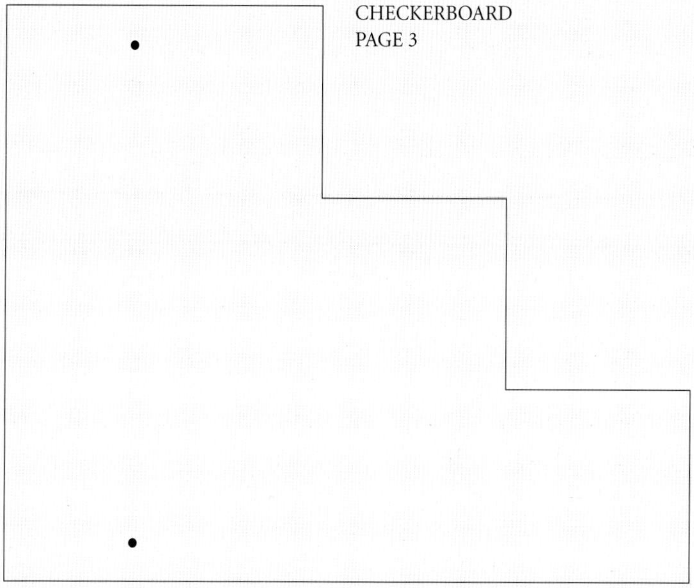

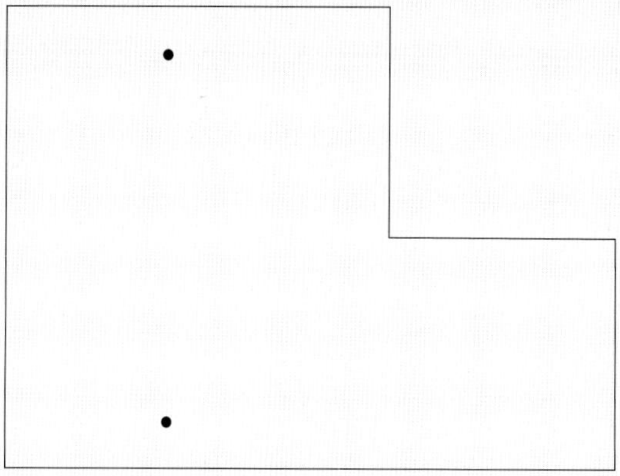

CHECKERBOARD PAGE 2

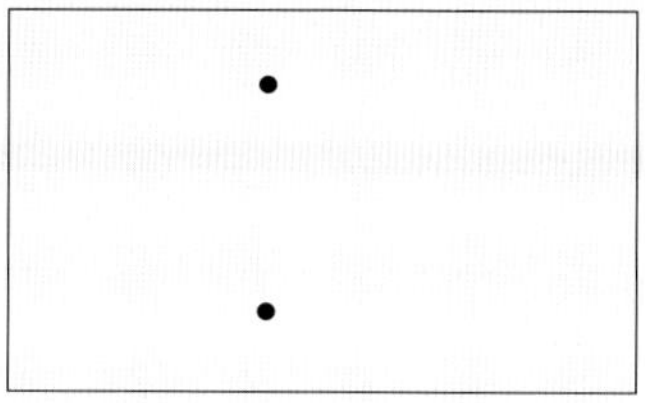

CHECKERBOARD PAGE 1

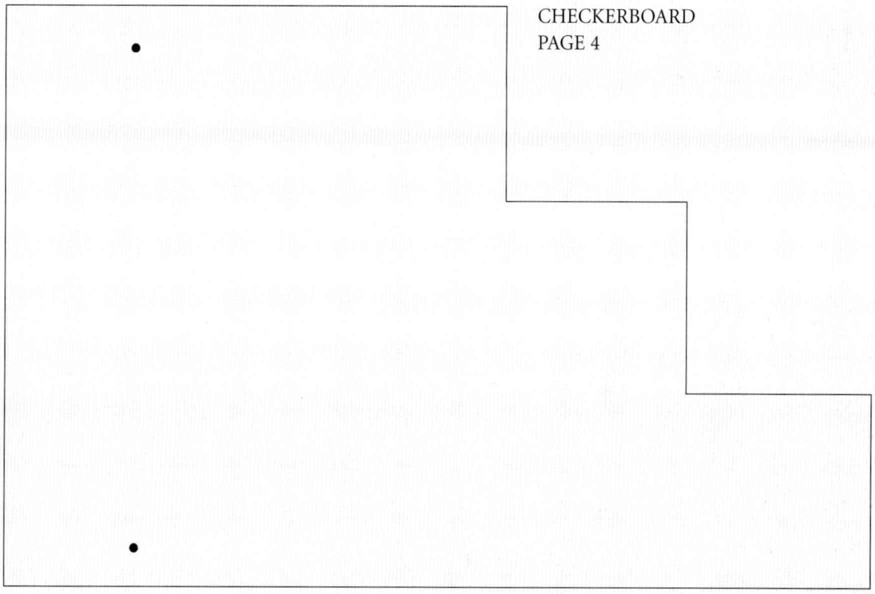

CHECKERBOARD
PAGE 3

CHECKERBOARD
PAGE 4

CHECKERBOARD
PAGE 5

CRISS-CROSS BOOK

TOOLS AND MATERIALS

basic tool kit (page 8)

BASE 5½" (14.0cm) square piece of mat-board

COVER FOR BASE 7" (17.8cm) square piece of decorative paper

LINER FOR BASE 5" (12.7cm) square piece of decorative paper

COVERS FOR FOUR BOOKS 7" × 11" (17.8cm × 27.9cm) piece of cardstock (grain long)

PAGES FOR FOUR BOOKS two 6¾" × 10" (17.1cm × 25.4cm) pieces of text paper (grain long)

SEWING STATION TEMPLATE 2½" × 5" (6.4cm × 12.7cm) piece of scrap card-stock (grain short)

> > ONE DAY, SEEKING INSPIRATION, I rummaged through a big box of models I had made for various projects. I pulled out four small books and started stacking and repositioning them. Bingo! Within minutes I had made a rough model for the Criss-Cross Book, which features four tiny overlapping books mounted to a single base. You can hang your Criss-Cross Book on the wall, or attach feet underneath the base and elevate your creation to the level of sculpture. Get creative and make hexagonal or octagonal bases with six or eight Criss-Cross Books!

1 COVER BASE

Cover and line matboard base, following directions on pages 13–14.

2 MEASURE AND MARK CARDSTOCK

Place the cardstock for the covers facedown in a horizontal position. Measuring from the left edge, draw light vertical pencil lines at $2\frac{3}{4}$" (7.0cm), $5\frac{1}{2}$" (14.0cm) and $8\frac{1}{4}$" (21.0cm). With the cardstock in a vertical position, measure over $3\frac{1}{2}$" (8.9cm) from the left edge and draw a light vertical pencil line. Valley score, fold and crease this line.

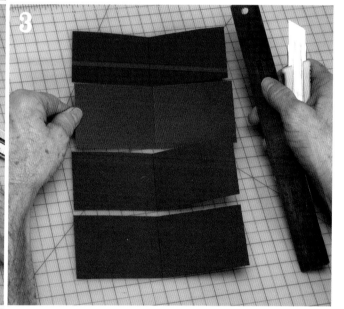

3 CUT CARDSTOCK

Open the cardstock and cut along the three horizontal lines to create four covers.

4 CREATE PAPER PAGES

Place one piece of text-weight paper in a horizontal position. Measuring over from the left edge, draw light vertical pencil lines at $2\frac{1}{2}$" (6.4cm), 5" (12.7cm) and $7\frac{1}{2}$" (19.1cm). Place the marked-up paper on top of the second piece of text-weight paper and square up the edges. Cut through both papers along the solid lines to create eight $2\frac{1}{2}$" × $7\frac{1}{2}$" (6.4cm × 19.1cm) rectangles.

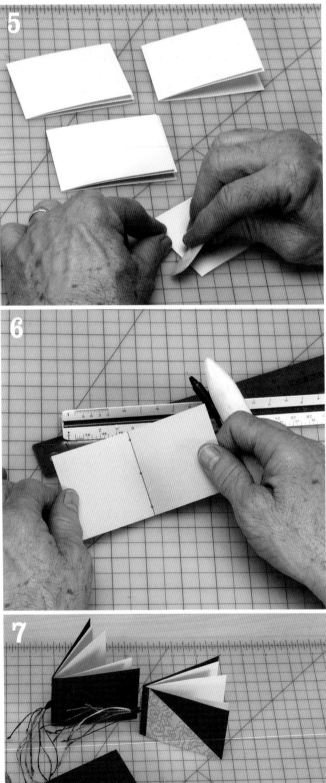

5 MAKE SECTIONS

Fold each rectangle in half and crease to create eight folios. Make four sections of two folios each, as shown.

6 MAKE SEWING STATION TEMPLATE

Place the sewing station template card-stock in a horizontal position. Pencil in a vertical line 2½" (6.4cm) from the left edge. Valley score, fold and crease the line. Then, measure down from the top edge and make pencil dots on the center fold at ¼" (6mm), 1¼" (3.2cm) and 2¼" (5.7cm).

7 ATTACH SECTIONS TO COVERS

Place one section inside one cover, centered head to tail. Insert the sewing station template and pierce three holes. Sew the section to the cover, with the knot on the outside, as described on page 15. Sew the remaining sections to the covers. Embellish the covers as desired, adding beads, threads, etc.

8 ATTACH FIRST TWO BOOKS

Books can be attached to either surface of the base in many configurations. First, apply glue to the outside surface of the back cover of one book, position the book on the base and burnish the cover in place. Apply glue to the back cover of the second book and attach it to the base over the inside surface of the cover of the first book. Burnish.

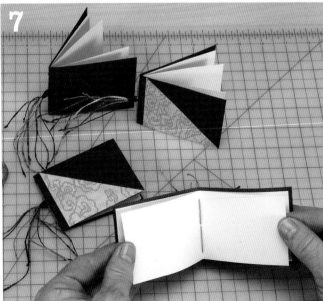

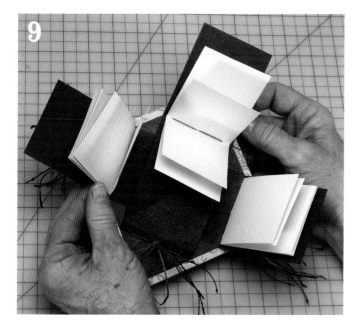

9 FINISH BOOK

Open the covers and pages of the first two books. Apply glue to the outside surface of the back cover of the third book and attach to the base over the inside surface of book cover two. Burnish. Attach book four to the base over the inside surface of book cover three. Burnish.

The books on this Criss-Cross Book variation are different sizes, glued to a rectangular base. The white bone bead acts as a cinch to keep the books closed.
CHALLENGE: Make a Criss-Cross Book with a base with no right angles!

ALTERNATE ENDINGS

LOLLIPOP STICK BOOK

TOOLS AND MATERIALS

basic tool kit (page 8)

measuring templates (page 51)

lollipop stick or ⅛" (3mm) dowel

COVER
7½" × 11" (19.1cm × 27.9cm) piece of card-stock (grain short)

BOOK BLOCK
7½" × 11" (19.1cm × 27.9cm) piece of card-stock (grain short)

OPTIONAL
hammer

eyelets

black marker

heart-shaped bead

> > I WAS CRUISING THE CONFECTIONERY SECTION of a craft store one day and noticed packages of white lollipop sticks. These pristine rolled paper sticks intrigued me and I decided to buy a package. I had no clue then that one of these sticks would become the major component of the binding for the Lollipop Stick Book! Measuring templates make this piano hinge book easy to construct, and the unique design allows you to remove the stick and swap positions with the cover and book block! Consider changing the size of the book or incorporating two book blocks at the spine.

1 MARK COVER CARDSTOCK USING TEMPLATE

Place the cover cardstock facedown in a horizontal position. Place the top edge of the cardstock just below the horizontal line on the cover template, with the left edge of the cardstock in line with the left end of the template. Transfer the marks on the template to the top edge of the cardstock. Then slide the cardstock up and place the bottom edge just above the horizontal line on the template, and transfer the marks to the bottom edge of the cover cardstock, as shown.

2 FOLD CARDSTOCK

Valley score, fold and crease the five vertical lines indicated by the pencil marks, working left to right.

3 MARK AND FOLD BOOK BLOCK CARDSTOCK

Place the cardstock for your book block facedown on your work surface. Transfer the marks on the book block template to the top and bottom edges of the cardstock, as you did for the cover in step 1. Valley fold and crease the five vertical lines, again working left to right.

4 FOLD TURN-INS

Fold the foredge turn-ins on the cover to the inside, then fold the cover in half.

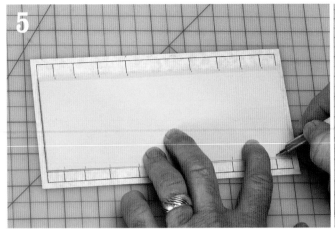

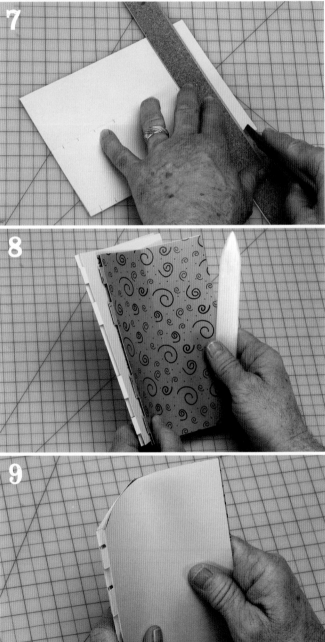

5 MARK COVER

Place the folded cover on top of the spine template with the left and right edges touching the sides of the template, centered top to bottom. Hold the cover in place and make tick marks at the top and bottom of the cover to match the vertical lines on the template, as shown above.

6 PLACE BOOK BLOCK INSIDE COVER

Open the turn-ins on the cover and book block. Place the folded book block inside the folded cover. Square up the cover and the book block.

7 CUT SPINE

Place the book block/cover unit in a horizontal position with the center fold at the bottom. Align the ruler on the first set of tick marks on the cover. Start the cut just a hair past the second fold and cut slits out through the center fold, penetrating the cover and the book block. Repeat with the remaining sets of tick marks. When finished, erase all pencil marks from the cover.

NOTE: *The slits are very short. The upper tick marks will help you position the ruler so the slits will be parallel to the top and bottom of the cover and book block.*

8 REVERSE SPINE SECTIONS

Remove the book block from the cover and reverse every other section on the cover and book block spine, as shown above. Place a clean piece of scrap paper over the folds and crease heavily.

9 FIT SPINES TOGETHER

Place the book block back inside the cover. Gently glide the slotted sections together and square up.

Cutting Out Interior Windows

I cut five windows in the cover of the Lollipop Stick Book to showcase the embellishments and parts of the book block. It is easy to accidentally overcut at the corners when cutting windows, since the blade of your knife is at an angle. The following technique creates windows with crisp corners and no overcutting.

FIRST, DRAW AND CUT LINES

Draw or trace the window shape onto your paper. Then, stab your knife point into the upper left corner, swing your ruler gently into the knife blade and align it with the pencil line. Cut along the line, stopping just short of the bottom corner. Remove your knife and repeat the cutting process on the remaining lines.

THEN, STAB CORNERS

Turn the paper over and lightly stab each attached corner with your knife in alignment with previous cuts. This stabbing action slices through the tiny bit of paper left at each corner, creating windows with crisp corners and no overcutting.

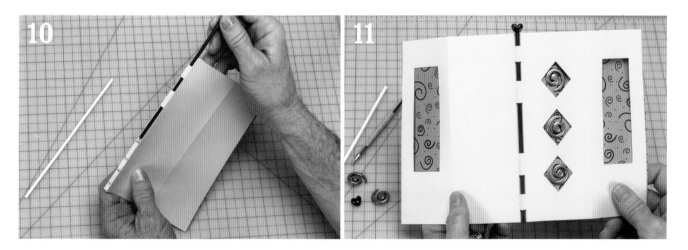

10 ADD STICK

Weave a lollipop stick (or dowel, glass or brass rod, etc.) alternately through the slits on the spine.

NOTE: *In the photo above, the lollipop stick being inserted into the spine slits has been dyed with a black marker.*

11 FINISH BOOK

Embellish the book as desired. I cut out windows, added decorative eyelets and glued a red heart-shaped bead to the top of the lollipop stick.

ADD SOME KICK!

It's super easy to radically change the look of this book without adding any additional components. Follow the steps at right and turn your book inside out!

Remove the lollipop stick and release the book block from the cover. Place the cover inside the book block and weave the lollipop stick back through the slits on the spine.

Fold in the turn-ins on the book block so the cover creates a narrow border at each foredge. CHALLENGE: Create text on both the cover and the book block that somehow makes sense no matter which component is on the outside!

ALTERNATE ENDINGS

The windows and frames in this Lollipop Stick Book variation can be rearranged to highlight different areas of the book block.
CHALLENGE: Create a Lollipop Stick Book with a wider book block.

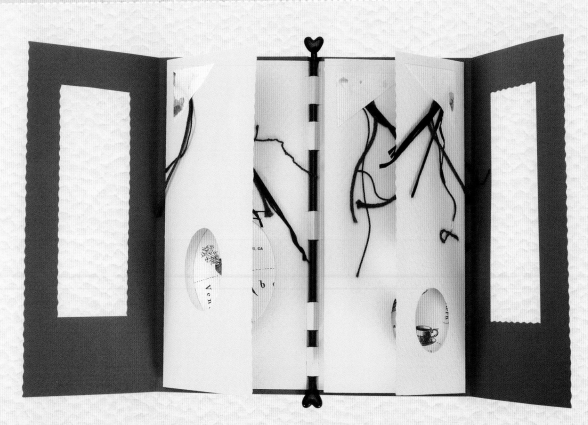

MEASURING TEMPLATES FOR LOLLIPOP STICK BOOK

Templates are full size. You will be using these templates to make measurements; to do so, you can work directly from this page, or you can photocopy this page for more-portable templates.

SPINE TEMPLATE FOR COVER AND BOOK BLOCK

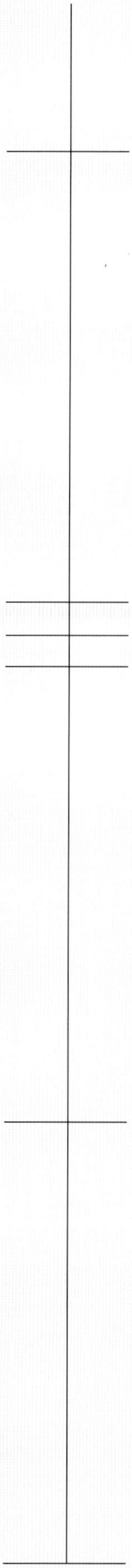

BOOK BLOCK TEMPLATE

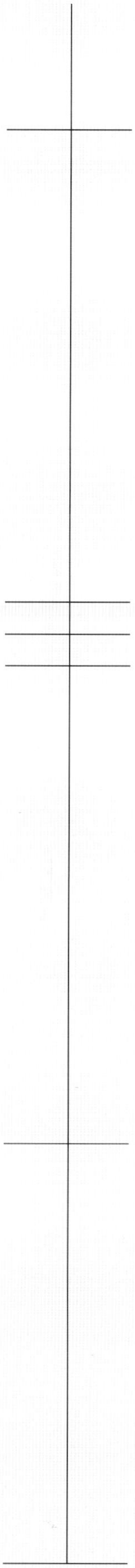

COVER TEMPLATE

PIANO HINGE JOURNAL

TOOLS AND MATERIALS

basic tool kit (page 8)

PIANO HINGE COVERS
two 6" × 8½" (15.2cm × 21.6cm) pieces of cardstock (grain short)

JOURNAL COVER
6" × 7¾" (15.2cm × 19.7cm) piece of cardstock (grain short)

PAGES
six 5¾" × 7¼" (14.6cm × 18.4cm) pieces of text paper (grain short)

OPTIONAL
alphabet rubber stamps

> > THE PIANO HINGE JOURNAL IS A REAL WORKHORSE. The cover is made from two identical units connected at the spine with a simple and elegant piano hinge. Tailor the covers for your destination—make separate pamphlet-stitched journals for Montego Bay, Port Antonio and Kingston, and you're ready for Jamaica! The piano hinge cover protects each journal, and the interchangeability aspect allows you to keep the whole thing manageable.

1 PREPARE FRONT COVER

Place the cardstock for the piano hinge front cover facedown in a horizontal position. Draw light vertical pencil lines 1" (2.5cm) and 5" (12.7cm) from the left edge. Write "front" lightly in pencil in the upper right corner.

2 MARK FRONT COVER

Measure down from the top edge and make tick marks at the left and right edges at 1" (2.5cm), 2" (5.1cm), 3" (7.6cm), 4" (10.2cm) and 5" (12.7cm). Line up the ruler on the pencil marks and draw horizontal lines starting at the left edge and ending at the first vertical line, as shown. Valley score both vertical lines. Fold and crease each score.

3 PREPARE BACK COVER

Repeat steps 1 and 2 with the cardstock for the piano hinge back cover. You may find it helpful to write "back" lightly in pencil in the upper right corner.

4 CUT COVERS

Cut out the first, third and fifth squares on each piano hinge cover, as shown. Erase the tick marks on the right edges of the covers.

5 APPLY GLUE TO FRONT COVER GLUE FLAPS

Run a glue stick over the inside surface of the piano hinge front cover glue flaps, using paper guards to protect the cover and work surface, as shown.

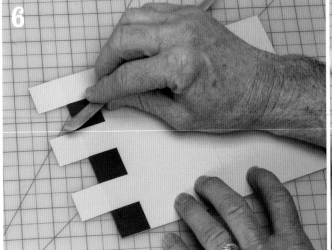

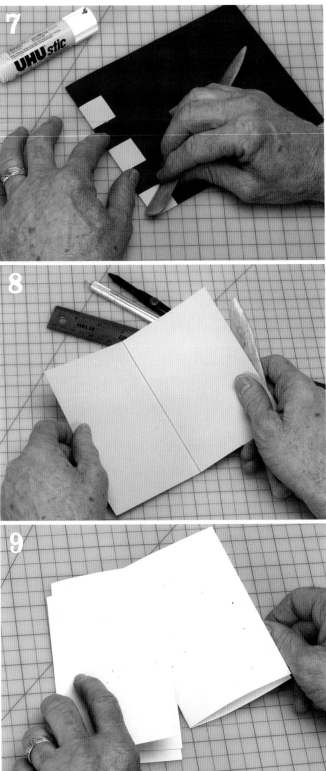

6 GLUE FRONT FLAPS TO BACK COVER

Remove the glue guards and place the inside surface of the piano hinge back cover on top of the inside surface of the piano hinge front cover. Square up the covers and fold the glue flaps on the front cover to the right. Burnish the flaps to the back cover.

7 GLUE BACK FLAPS TO FRONT COVER

Flip the cover unit over top to bottom. Using glue guards to protect the front cover and work surface, run a glue stick over the three glue flaps on the back cover. Remove the glue guards, fold the flaps to the right and burnish them to the front cover. Open the covers and erase the words "front" and "back."

8 PREPARE JOURNAL COVER

Place the cardstock for the journal cover facedown in a horizontal position. Measure over $3\frac{7}{8}$" (9.8cm) from the left edge and draw a vertical pencil line down the center. Valley score, fold and crease the line.

9 CREATE SECTION

Fold six page papers in half, parallel to the grain (the fold will run parallel to the $5\frac{3}{4}$" (14.6cm) height). Crease all the folds, then place the folios inside each other to form a 24-page section.

10 SEW SECTION TO JOURNAL COVER

Sew the section to the inside fold of the journal cover (for instructions, see page 15). Insert the front and back covers of the journal under the turn-ins on the front and back of the piano hinge cover.

11 CREATE MORE JOURNALS

Create additional interchangeable journals to fit inside the piano hinge cover and embellish as desired. I rubber stamped titles on the front of each journal. By cutting a window in the front of the piano hinge cover, the large title letters provide a decorative focal point.

ALTERNATE ENDINGS

Covers can be made in any size with any number of piano hinges on the spine. The cover here has seven piano hinges in four graduated sizes. Use the interchangeable journals as grocery lists, address books, telephone message books and much more.

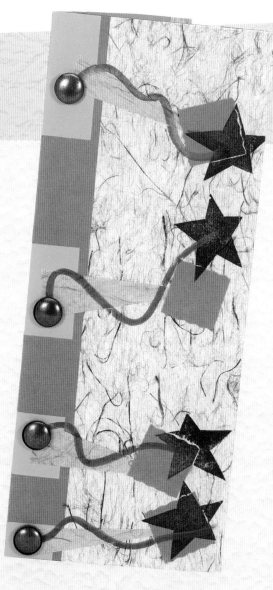

WRAP-AROUND JOURNAL

TOOLS AND MATERIALS

basic tool kit (page 8)

INNER COVER
8½" × 11" (21.6cm × 27.9cm) piece of cardstock (grain short)

OUTER COVER
8½" × 11" (21.6cm × 27.9cm) piece of cardstock (grain short)

PAGES
eight 8¼" (21.0cm) text-paper squares

SEWING STATION TEMPLATE
8¼" × 4" (21.0cm × 10.2cm) piece of scrap cardstock (grain long)

PORTFOLIO
8¼" × 11" (21.0cm × 27.9cm) piece of cardstock (grain short)

PORTFOLIO FLAPS
4¼" × 9" (10.8cm × 22.9cm) piece of cardstock (grain long)

> > IT BUGS ME THAT MANY SMALL JOURNALS ARE HARD TO WRITE IN NEAR THE SPINE. The Wrap-Around Journal is designed so the various components can be folded out of the way to create a flat surface when writing or sketching. And, you can modify this journal to suit your needs—make the journal in larger or smaller sizes, or leave out the portfolio and sew a third section to the valley fold at the far right.

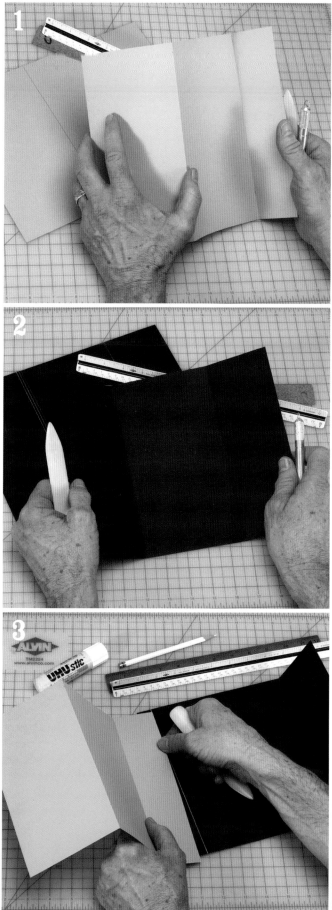

1 PREPARE INNER COVER

Place the cardstock for the inner cover facedown in a horizontal position. Measuring from the left edge, make tick marks at 4⅜" (11.1cm) and 8⅞" (22.5cm) at the top and bottom edges. Mountain score at 4⅜" (11.1cm) and valley score at 8⅞" (22.5cm). Fold and crease scores.

NOTE: *The inner cover will not show when the wrap-around journal is closed.*

2 PREPARE OUTER COVER

Place the cardstock for the outer cover facedown in a horizontal position. Measuring from the left edge, make tick marks at 3⅛" (7.9cm), 3¼" (8.3cm), 3⅜" (8.6cm) and 8" (20.3cm). Valley score each line indicated by the tick marks. Fold and crease each score. The first three scores create a *capacity fold* (see *Tip* on page 86 for definition and instructions on making capacity folds).

3 ATTACH INNER AND OUTER COVERS

With the outer cover facedown in a horizontal position and the capacity fold on the left side, draw a vertical pencil line ¾" (19mm) from the left edge. Run a glue stick over the ¾" (19mm) strip. Hold the inner cover facedown and attach the right edge of the smaller panel to the outer cover at the pencil line. Burnish.

4 MAKE FOLIOS

Fold eight page papers in half parallel to the grain to create eight folios. Make two sections with four folios in each section.

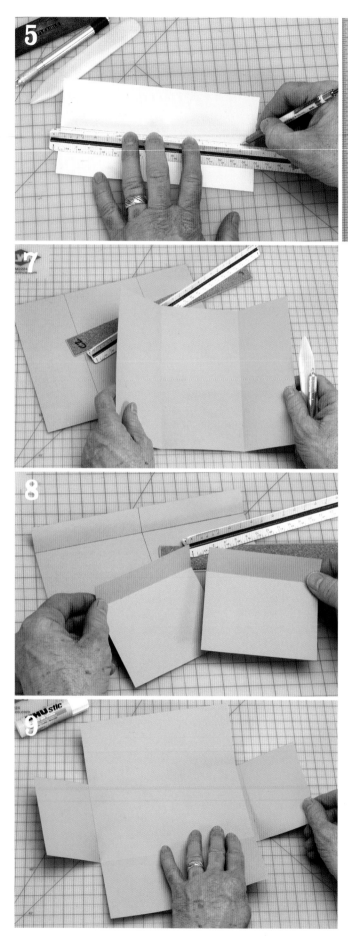

5 MAKE SEWING STATION TEMPLATE

Valley score down the middle of the sewing station template and place the template in a horizontal position. Measuring from the left edge, make pencil marks on the center fold at $5/8$" (16mm), $2^3/8$" (6.0cm), $4^1/8$" (10.5cm), $5^7/8$" (14.9cm) and $7^5/8$" (19.4cm).

6 SEW SECTION TO INNER COVER

Open the wrap-around cover and place it facedown in a horizontal position, with the inner cover on the left. Place one section in the valley fold on the inner cover and use the sewing station template to pierce five holes. Sew the section to the cover with the knot on the inside (for instructions, see page 15). Flip the cover unit over and sew the second section to the left valley fold, as shown.

7 SCORE AND CREASE PORTFOLIO CARDSTOCK

Place portfolio cardstock facedown in a horizontal position. Draw light vertical pencil lines $3^1/4$" (8.3cm) and $7^3/4$ (19.7cm) from the left edge. Valley score, fold and crease each line. Erase pencil lines.

8 MAKE PORTFOLIO FLAPS

Place the cardstock for portfolio flaps facedown in a horizontal position. Draw a light horizontal pencil line 1" (2.5cm) from top. Valley score, fold and crease the line. Measure $4^1/2$" (11.4cm) from the left edge and make tick marks at the top and bottom edges. Align the ruler on the tick marks and cut the cardstock in half to create two portfolio flaps.

9 ATTACH PORTFOLIO FLAPS

Place the portfolio facedown in a vertical position. Run a glue stick over the narrow glue strips on the inside surface of the flaps and attach them to the back of the portfolio on the left and right sides, centered between the horizontal folds. Burnish the flaps to the portfolio.

10 TRIM PORTFOLIO FLAPS

Trim pie-shaped wedges from the sides of the large top and bottom flaps, and from the top and bottom edges of the smaller side flaps. This will make the portfolio flaps easier to open and close. Decorate the portfolio as desired.

11 GLUE PORTFOLIO TO COVER

Close the flaps on the portfolio and run a glue stick over the outside surface of the middle section. Attach the portfolio to the inside panel on the outer cover, centered on all sides, as shown. Open the flaps and burnish the portfolio to the cover. Shape the flap on the outer cover and decorate covers as desired.

ALTERNATE ENDINGS

This Wrap-Around Journal was decorated with a map showcasing European countries visited. The portfolio inside this journal was sewn in place rather than glued, which allows it to swing out of the way when you are writing.
CHALLENGE: Design a Wrap-Around Journal (with a portfolio) that is 6" (15.2cm) square when closed.

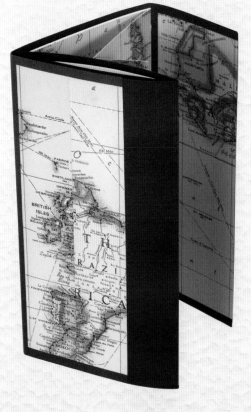

FOLDING JOURNAL

TOOLS AND MATERIALS

basic tool kit (page 8)

brads

marker

FOLDING CASE
six 4½" × 5" (11.4cm × 12.7cm)
pieces of matboard (grain long)

COVER PAPERS FOR FOLDING CASE
two 6" × 6½" (15.2cm × 16.5cm)
pieces of decorative paper
(grain long)

PORTFOLIOS
two 8½" × 11" (21.6cm × 27.9cm)
pieces of cardstock (grain short)

SMALL BOOK COVERS
two 3⅛" × 7" (7.9cm × 17.8cm)
pieces of cardstock (grain short)

PAGES FOR SMALL BOOKS
four 5¾" × 6¾" (14.6cm × 17.1cm)
pieces of text paper (grain short)

JOURNAL COVER
4¾" × 8½" (12.1cm × 21.6cm)
piece of cardstock (grain short)

PAGES FOR JOURNAL
three 8⅛" × 9" (20.6cm × 22.9cm)
pieces of text paper (grain long)

HINGE
1½" × 4½" (3.8cm × 11.4cm) piece
of cardstock (grain long)

> > THE FOLDING JOURNAL HAS EVERYTHING YOU NEED in a compact travel companion—one removable journal, two portfolios for tickets and receipts, and two small books tucked into side pockets to record travel expenses and addresses of the new friends you meet on your adventures. It folds in half to easily fit inside your purse, shoulder bag or backpack. It is easy to make, so don't leave home without one!

1 COVER BOARDS
Cover two matboard rectangles for the folding case with decorative cover papers (for instructions, see pages 13–14). Do not line these boards.

2 CUT REMAINING MATBOARD
Place one uncovered matboard rectangle in a vertical position. Draw horizontal lines $^7/_8$" (22mm) from the top and bottom edges and a vertical line $^7/_8$" (22mm) from the left edge. Cut out and recycle the center section. Repeat the process with one more uncovered matboard rectangle.

3 DYE AND GLUE MATBOARD PIECES
Use a marker to dye all the edges of the four uncovered matboard pieces, including the inside edges on the C-shaped pieces cut in step 2. Glue the C-shaped pieces to the plain matboard rectangles and burnish.

4 GLUE COVERS TO MATBOARD UNITS
Place one C-shape with the opening facing right and the other C-shape below it with the opening facing left. Spread craft glue or PVA over the top C-shape. Place the unlined side of one covered matboard on top of the C-shape, square up and burnish. Place under a weight for a few minutes until the glue is dry. Repeat the process with the remaining (bottom) C-shape.

5 CREATE FIRST PORTFOLIO
Place one sheet of portfolio cardstock facedown in a vertical position. Draw vertical lines 2" (5.1cm) and 6$^1/_2$" (16.5cm) from the left edge. Then, draw horizontal lines 1$^3/_4$" (4.4cm) and 6$^3/_4$" (17.1cm) down from the top edge. Cut out the corners and shape the flaps. Trace the portfolio shape to a second sheet of cardstock and cut out. Valley score, fold and crease four lines on each portfolio, then erase the pencil lines. Decorate portfolios as desired.

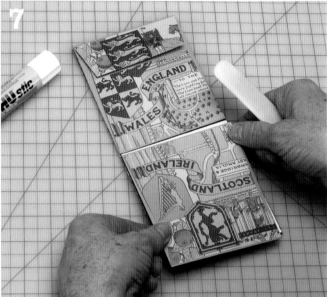

6 CREATE AND ATTACH HINGE

Place hinge cardstock faceup in a vertical position and valley score, fold and crease down the center. Butt matboard units together with the pocket in the top unit facing right and the pocket in the bottom unit facing left. Run a glue stick or brush PVA over the back of the hinge and attach it directly over the seam where the covers meet. Close the covers and square up if necessary. Open the covers and burnish the hinge to the covers.

7 ATTACH PORTFOLIOS

Flip the hinged matboard units over and place them on your work surface with the top pocket facing left and the bottom pocket facing right. Close the four flaps on one portfolio and run a glue stick or brush PVA over the back surface. Attach the portfolio to the upper matboard unit with the small flap at the top. Burnish. Attach the second portfolio to the lower matboard unit with the small flap at the bottom. Burnish. Set aside.

8 CREATE JOURNAL

Cut out the cover and page components for the journal. Valley score the cover down the center on the inside surface, then fold and crease the score. Cut text papers in half horizontally, fold each piece in half, and stack all six folios inside each other to make a 24-page section. Sew the section to the cover, with the knot on the inside (for instructions, see page 15).

9 CREATE SMALL BOOKS

Cut out the covers and page components for the two small books. Valley score each cover down the center, then fold and crease the scores. Cut page papers in half horizontally, fold each piece in half, and make two sections of four folios each. Center one section inside one cover and pierce three holes. Sew the section to the cover, with the knot on the outside (for instructions, see page 15). Repeat with the second cover and section. Decorate the covers if desired.

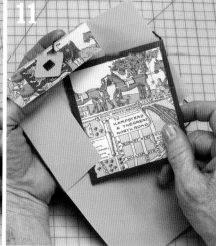

10 ADD TWO-BUTTON TIE
Add buttons to the flaps on each portfolio and tie a sturdy string behind one button (for instructions on making button-tie closures, see page 23).

11 INSERT JOURNAL
Insert the journal inside one of the portfolios.

12 INSERT SMALL BOOKS
Close both portfolios and fold the case in half. Wrap string around the case and each button to keep the case closed. Insert the two small books into the side pockets on the case.

ALTERNATE ENDINGS

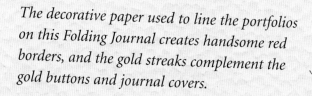

The decorative paper used to line the portfolios on this Folding Journal creates handsome red borders, and the gold streaks complement the gold buttons and journal covers.

FOUR UNDER COVER

TOOLS AND MATERIALS

basic tool kit (page 8)

beads, decorative thread and other embellishments

BASE
two 6¾" (17.1cm) matboard squares

COVER PAPERS
two 8¼" (21.0cm) decorative paper squares

LINERS
two 6½" (16.5cm) decorative paper squares

PAGES FOR FOUR BOOKS
three 5¼" × 10" (13.3cm × 25.4cm) pieces of text paper (grain long)

COVERS FOR FOUR BOOKS
5½" × 11" (14.0cm × 27.9cm) piece of cardstock (grain long)

SEWING STATION TEMPLATE
3" × 2½" (7.6cm × 6.4cm) piece of scrap cardstock (grain short)

SPACERS
1" × 6½" (2.5cm × 16.5cm) piece of matboard

two 1" × 2¾" (2.5cm × 7.0cm) pieces of matboard

OPTIONAL
four objects for feet

> > EVERY ONCE IN A WHILE, I'LL NAME A BOOK SCULPTURE FIRST, and then use the name as inspiration to design the book. This is how the Four Under Cover came to be. The structure hides a book in each corner pocket, with threads on the spines so you can easily remove them. The Four Under Cover is complete in itself, or it can be the starting point for amazing and complex book sculptures. Challenge yourself to design a book that fits its name!

1 PREPARE BOTTOM OF BASE

Cover and line one matboard square (for instructions, see pages 13–14). With the liner faceup and the grain running vertically, draw an arrow in the upper right corner to indicate grain direction. Draw vertical lines 2⅞" (7.3cm) and 3⅞" (9.8cm) from the left edge. Then draw horizontal lines 2⅞" (7.3cm) and 3⅞" (9.8cm) from the top.

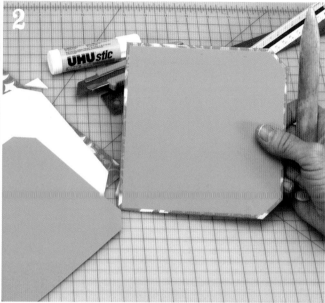

2 PREPARE TOP OF BASE

Place the second matboard square on your work surface with the grain running vertically. Cut off ¾" (19mm) triangular sections from the top and bottom corners on the right side. Cover and line the board (for instructions, see pages 13–14), with the grain on all components running vertically. Draw an arrow in the upper right corner to indicate the grain direction (arrow not shown in photo).

3 GLUE SPACERS IN PLACE

Place the covered board from step 1 on your work surface, with the liner faceup. Coat one surface of the long matboard spacer with craft glue or PVA and burnish it in place between the vertical lines, centered top to bottom. Glue and burnish the short matboard spacers to the left and right sides of the long spacer between pencil lines, as shown.

4 COMPLETE BASE

Coat the top surface of the spacers with craft glue or PVA. Attach the covered board with clipped corners to the spacers with the liner facedown and the arrows on each board running parallel. Place a weight on top of the boards for about 15 minutes, until the glue is dry.

5 MAKE FOLIOS
Fold page papers in half vertically and crease the folds. Open each paper and smooth it out. Measuring down from the top of one paper, draw light pencil lines at 2½" (6.4cm), 5" (12.7cm) and 7½" (19.1cm). Stack and square up the papers, with the marked paper on top. Cut through the lines to make four small sections with three folios in each section.

6 MAKE BOOK COVERS
Place the book cover cardstock facedown in a vertical position. Measuring over 2¾" (7.0cm) from the left edge, draw a light vertical pencil line. Then, measuring down from the top, draw horizontal lines at 2¾" (7.0cm), 5½" (14.0cm) and 8¼" (21cm). Valley score, fold and crease the vertical line. Then, cut along the pencil lines to create four book covers.

7 SEW BOOKS
Place the sewing station template cardstock horizontally, then score vertically down the center. Fold and crease score. Make three dots on the center fold to indicate sewing stations. Using the sewing station template, pierce three holes through four sections and covers, as shown.

8 DECORATE COVERS
Sew sections in place with the knots on the outside (for instructions, see page 15). Tie beads and other embellishments to the threads, then trim to desired length. Decorate covers if desired.

9 ADD FEET AND INSERT BOOKS
Glue four feet to the bottom of the base (the covered matboard with all four corners intact). Flip over and insert the four books, foredge first, into the corner pockets. The threads at the center of each book spine act as pulls to remove the books from the pockets.

ADD SOME KICK!

The "guts" of this rectangular Seven Under Cover structure hint at countless possibilities!

As you can see from the "guts," the outer ends of the spacers have been wrapped with decorative paper, and the spacers at the top are angled to create corner pockets for two triangle books. Part of the vertical middle spacer was left out to create a side-to-side pocket for a long, narrow book.

I glued six feet to the bottom of the Seven Under Cover base to prevent sagging. Shapes of the seven books shown at left include triangles, rectangles and squares.

Once your structure is complete, think about ways to combine multiple structures. Consider layering several under cover structures for an architectural look, or hinging three or more structures accordion style to create a mega-pocket structure.

ALTERNATE ENDINGS

This *Four Under Cover* variation was made from cardstock squares. I cut the finished base in half through the vertical spacer, then cut the right half in half through the horizontal spacer. I joined the three sections back together with a vertical cardstock hinge, and sewed the hinge to a cardstock cover with a capacity fold. This *Four Under Cover* structure folds in half and fits snugly inside a slipcase, which I made with a paper ruler.

PICTURE FRAME BOOK

TOOLS AND MATERIALS

basic tool kit (page 8)

marker

WINDOW FRAMES
four 3" × 5" (7.6cm × 12.7cm) pieces of matboard (grain long)

COVER PAPERS
four 4" × 6" (10.2cm × 15.2cm) pieces of decorative paper (grain long)

LINERS
four 2½" × 4½" (6.4cm × 11.4cm) pieces of decorative paper (grain long)

HINGES
three ½" × 4½" (13mm × 11.4cm) pieces of cardstock (grain long)

PAGES
2¾" × 11" (7.0cm × 27.9cm) piece of cardstock (grain short)

POCKETS
2¼" × 9" (5.7cm × 22.9cm) piece of cardstock (grain short)

> > THE DRAWING FOR A BOOK STRUCTURE BASED ON A PICTURE FRAME waited patiently in my sketchbook for three years before I brought it to three-dimensional life. After many models and much fine-tuning, I created the Picture Frame Book. Mini picture frames hold tiny books, loose pages or small objects. The frames can be hinged together to make an accordion-fold book, or joined in a zigzag manner to create a playful itinerary through the text. A custom-fitted box, made with a paper ruler, houses and protects this interactive book.

1 COVER MATBOARD

Cover and line all four matboard rectangles (for instructions, see pages 13–14).

2 CREATE PICTURE FRAME PATTERN

Cut out a 3" × 5" (7.6cm × 12.7cm) rectangle from scrap cardstock. Draw a rectangular window in the center, $\frac{3}{4}$" (19mm) from the top, bottom and sides. Cut out the window (for instructions, see page 49). Set the cutout piece aside.

3 CREATE TWO PICTURE FRAMES

Place the picture frame pattern over the liner on two matboards and trace the opening. With a utility knife and the cork side of your ruler facedown for safety, cut out the center areas. Dye the inside edges of the two picture frames with a marker.

4 CREATE POCKET SQUARES

Place the pocket cardstock faceup in a horizontal position. Measuring over from the left edge, draw light pencil lines at $2\frac{1}{4}$" (5.7cm), $4\frac{1}{2}$" (11.4cm) and $6\frac{3}{4}$" (17.1cm). Cut through the lines to create four $2\frac{1}{4}$" (5.7cm) pocket squares. If desired, dye the edges of the squares with a marker.

5 ATTACH FRONT POCKET SQUARE

Run the glue stick down the sides and along the bottom of one pocket square, keeping the glue swath to $\frac{1}{4}$" (6mm) in width. Attach the pocket square to the liner side of one picture frame with a $\frac{1}{8}$" (3mm) border formed by the liner. Burnish.

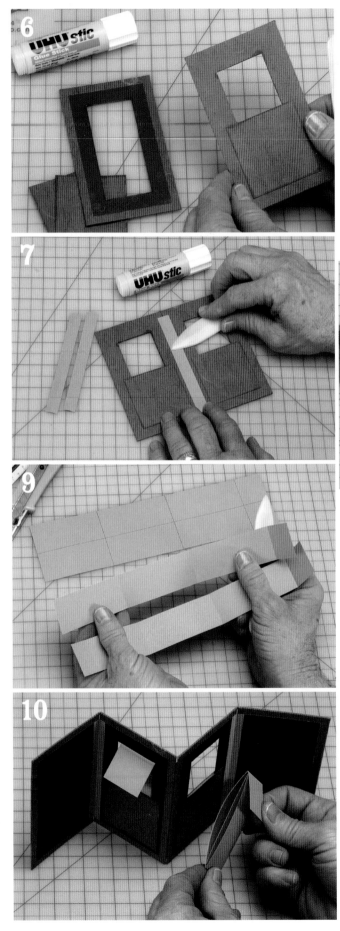

6 ATTACH BACK POCKET SQUARE

Attach a second pocket square on the back side of the picture frame directly over the first pocket square. Burnish. Repeat steps 5 and 6 with the remaining picture frame and two pocket squares.

7 ATTACH BACK HINGE

Place hinge pieces faceup in a vertical position. Valley score, fold and crease the center of each hinge. Place two picture frames side by side with the liners face-down. Run a glue stick over the back surface of one hinge and attach it directly over the seam at the middle of the picture frames. Burnish the hinge in place, as shown.

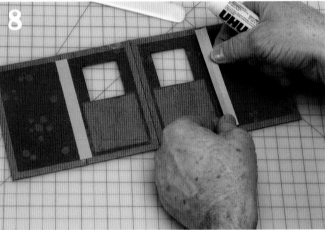

8 ATTACH FRONT HINGES

Flip the hinged picture frames over with the pockets at the bottom. Place one covered matboard next to the left picture frame. Glue up the second hinge and attach it to the covered matboard and the picture frame along the seam. Burnish the hinge in place. Glue up the third hinge and join the remaining covered matboard to the picture frame on the right in a similar manner.

9 CUT PAGES

Place the page cardstock facedown in a horizontal position. Draw a light horizontal pencil line $1^{3}/_{8}$" (3.5cm) from the top. Measure over from the left edge and valley score at $3^{1}/_{8}$" (7.9cm), $6^{3}/_{8}$" (16.2cm) and $9^{3}/_{4}$" (24.8cm). Fold and crease all scores. Cut along horizontal line to create two pages.

10 PLACE PAGES IN POCKETS

Fold the two pages at the scores and place them in the pockets, as shown. Embellish the pages, window frames and outer panels as desired. To keep the book closed, make a sleeve (for instructions, see pages 17–18) or construct a custom-fitted box (for instructions, see pages 18–20).

ADD SOME KICK!

This larger Picture Frame Book features silk liners around the window openings and pages with button ties. The beautiful paste paper used to cover the boards (see the third image below) was created by artist Rhiannon Dent and given to me at a workshop in her home state of New Mexico.

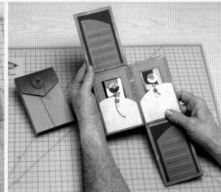

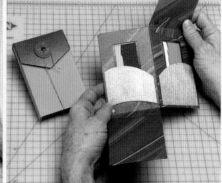

The two center panels are hinged on the front and fold forward. I used a paper ruler to make the box and added a button to the flap and to each page.

The solid panels hinged to the top left and bottom right picture frames fold backwards, and the curves at the tops of the text panels reflect the shapes at the tops of the pockets and help unify the design.

This back view shows the curved shape of the hinges and the paste paper used to cover the boards.

ALTERNATE ENDINGS

This five-panel Picture Frame Book is lined with vibrant watercolor paper, handpainted by Texas artist Maggie Gillikin. Regardless of the number of panels hinged together, the "footprint" remains the size of a single panel.

CONCERTINA CABARET

>> OVER THE YEARS, I HAVE MADE CONCERTINA BOOKS in many shapes and sizes. The Concertina Cabaret, with its square matboard covers, is my all-time favorite (so far!). When the structure is removed from its slipcase and fully extended, it is transformed into a freestanding, tactile sculpture with five inter-active pages. You can easily increase the length of the expandable spine and include more interactive pages of your own design.

1 COVER MATBOARD

Cover both 5" (12.7cm) matboard squares with 6½" (16.5cm) square cover papers and line with 4⅞" (12.4cm) square liner papers (for instructions, see pages 13–14).

2 PREPARE SPINE

Place the concertina spine cardstock facedown in a horizontal position. Measuring from the left, draw light pencil lines at 1" (2.5cm), 2" (5.1cm), 3" (7.6cm), 4" (10.2cm), 5" (12.7cm), 6" (15.2cm) and 7" (17.8cm). Valley score lines 1, 3, 5 and 7, then crease each score. Mountain score lines 2, 4 and 6, then crease each score. Trim ¼" (6mm) from each corner.

3 MAKE SEWING STATION TEMPLATE

Place the scrap cardstock for the sewing station template in a vertical position. Measure over 1¼" (3.2cm) from the left edge and draw a vertical line down the center of the template. Valley score, fold and crease the line. Open the template and make pencil marks on the center line ½" (13mm), 2½" (6.4cm) and 4½" (11.4cm) from the top edge.

4 MAKE PORTHOLE INSERT (INSERT A)

Place the porthole cardstock facedown in a horizontal position. Measuring from the left edge, draw vertical lines at 3¾" (9.5cm) and 7⅝" (19.4cm). Valley score, fold and crease each line. Use a circle cutter to cut a porthole in the upper center portion of the left panel, as shown.

5 MAKE PORTFOLIO INSERT (INSERT B)

Place the portfolio cardstock facedown in a vertical position. Draw horizontal lines 1$^3/_8$" (3.5cm) and 6$^1/_4$" (15.9cm) from the top edge. Draw vertical lines 1$^3/_4$" (4.4cm) and 6$^3/_4$" (17.1cm) from the left edge. Cut away four corner areas. Shape each flap if desired, as I've done here. Valley score all four lines, then fold and crease.

6 MAKE BOOK INSERT (INSERT C)

Place the book cardstock facedown in a horizontal position. Measuring from the left edge, draw a vertical line at 3$^7/_8$" (9.8cm). Valley score along the line, then fold and crease the score. Place page papers for the book insert horizontally and fold them in half from left to right. Crease the folds. Stack the folios inside each other to create a 12-page section, place the section inside the book insert, and set aside.

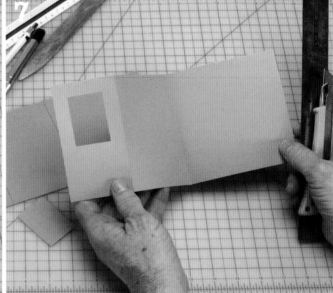

7 MAKE FRAME INSERT (INSERT D)

Place the frame cardstock facedown in a horizontal position. Draw vertical lines 2$^3/_4$" (7.0cm) and 6$^1/_8$" (15.6cm) from the left edge. Mountain score the first line and valley score the second line. Fold and crease each score. Cut an opening in the top center of the narrow panel (for instructions, see page 49). The window here has $^5/_8$" (16mm) borders at left, top and fold, and the bottom is 2$^1/_4$" (5.7cm) from the bottom edge.

8 MAKE EXPANDABLE FOREDGE INSERT (INSERT E)

Place the expandable foredge cardstock facedown in a horizontal position. Draw vertical lines $^7/_8$" (22mm), 4$^3/_4$" (12.1cm), 5$^3/_4$" (14.6cm) and 6$^3/_4$" (17.1cm) from the left edge. Mountain score the 5$^3/_4$" (14.6cm) line and valley score the three remaining lines. Fold and crease all the scores.

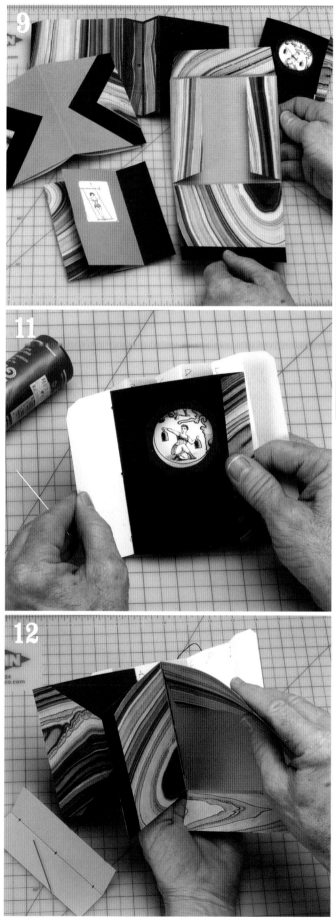

9 DECORATE INSERTS

Glue or tape a photo, drawing or text behind the window openings on the porthole and frame inserts, and decorate the inside and outside surfaces of each insert as desired.

10 PIERCE HOLES IN SPINE

Place the concertina spine facedown in a horizontal position (the left and right edges will be raised). Starting at the first mountain fold on the left, write letters A, B, C, D and E on the folds. Place the sewing station template in valley folds B and D, and pierce three holes in each fold, as shown. Flip the concertina spine over and use the sewing template to pierce three holes in each of the three valley folds. Flip the spine over again to the inside surface, with the letter A at the top left.

11 ATTACH PORTHOLE INSERT

Open the porthole insert (insert A) with the inside surface up and the window at top left. Place the sewing template in the left valley fold and pierce three holes. Remove the template and sew the porthole insert to mountain fold A on the concertina spine (for instructions, see page 15). The thread ends may be hidden on the inside of the fold or exposed at the spine. Glue the small flap at right to the outside or inside of the porthole insert. Burnish.

12 ATTACH PORTFOLIO INSERT

Open the portfolio insert (insert B) with the inside surface up and the largest flap facing left. Place the sewing template in the left valley fold and pierce three holes. Remove the template and sew the portfolio insert to valley fold B on the concertina spine (for instructions, see page 15).

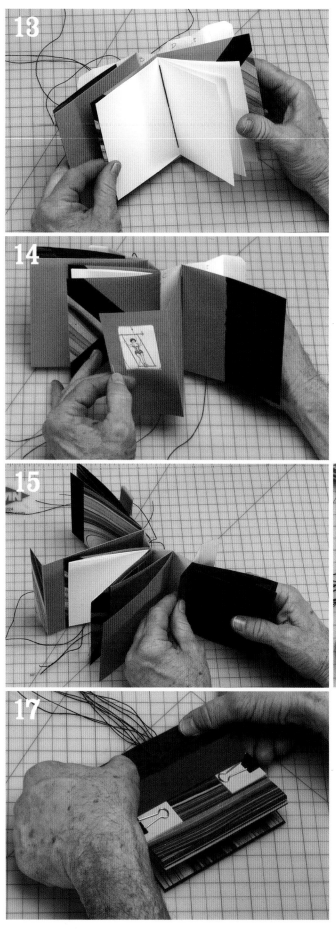

13 ATTACH BOOK INSERT

Open the book insert (insert C) and section. Place the sewing template inside the centermost fold of the section. Pierce three holes through the section and spine of the book insert cover. Remove the template and sew the book insert to mountain fold C on the concertina spine (for instructions, see page 15).

14 ATTACH FRAME INSERT

Open the frame insert (insert D) with the inside surface up and the window at top left. Place the sewing template in the valley fold and pierce three holes. Remove the template and sew the frame insert to valley fold D on the concertina spine (for instructions, see page 15).

15 ATTACH EXPANDABLE FOREDGE INSERT

Open the expandable foredge insert (insert E) with the inside surface up and the smallest section facing left. Place the sewing template in the left valley fold and pierce three holes. Remove the template and sew the insert to mountain fold E on the concertina spine (for instructions, see page 15). Collapse the insert as shown, then glue and burnish the small flap to the front of the insert. Erase all letters.

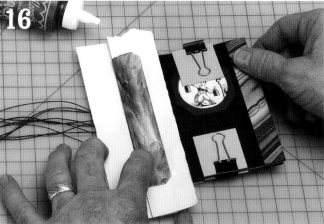

16 APPLY GLUE

Close all inserts and hold them closed with clips over small pieces of matboard. Position the insert unit with the porthole insert on top and the ends of the concertina spine facing left. Fold the top section of the spine to the right and coat the outer surface with craft glue or PVA, using glue guards to protect the insert.

17 ATTACH FRONT COVER

Remove the glue guards and turn the insert unit over. Attach the spine section to the inside surface of the front cover with all edges on both components flush. Burnish the spine to the front cover.

18 ATTACH BACK COVER

Flip the insert/cover unit over and coat the remaining spine section with craft glue or PVA. Attach the spine section to the inside of the back cover with all edges on the front and back covers flush. Burnish the spine to the back cover.

19 CREATE SLEEVE

Construct a custom-fitted sleeve (see pages 17–18) or box (see pages 18–20) to house the Concertina Cabaret book. Embellish the book and slipcover as desired.

ALTERNATE ENDINGS

This colorful Concertina Cabaret was decorated with inexpensive wrapping paper. The center insert contains sections sewn inside French doors.
CHALLENGE: Make a Concertina Cabaret with throwouts on each page!

BEYOND COVERED BOARDS

> > THE SCULPTURAL BOOK WORKS IN THIS second section are grouped loosely into three categories—Boxes With Books, Modular Books and Wired Books. In this section, you'll learn how to make:

* books with pockets and hidden compartments
* a book and miniature display case with an airtight clear polyfilm window
* an expandable album with a smooth-as-silk, wire-edge hinge
* versatile structures with fantastic text possibilities and triangular sides that turn inside out
* collapsible house-shaped structures with stilts and roof-books
* an interactive book in its own portfolio case

I hope you enjoy these last nine sculptural books. Add feet, legs and risers to turn them into awesome sculptures. Look at these projects as exercises to stimulate creative skills, and consider them a springboard for new book formats of your own design! The key word is *experimentation*.

MATCHBOX MARVEL

TOOLS AND MATERIALS

basic tool kit (page 8)

pattern (page 81)

three small matchboxes

one round toothpick

multicolored string

acrylic paint or stain

paintbrush

TOP AND BOTTOM
two $2^{1}/_{4}$" × $4^{1}/_{2}$" (5.7cm × 11.4cm)
pieces of matboard (grain long)

COVER PAPERS
two $3^{1}/_{4}$" × $5^{1}/_{2}$" (8.3cm × 14.0cm)
pieces of decorative paper
(grain long)

PYRAMID
$4^{1}/_{2}$" × 8" (11.4cm × 20.3cm) piece
of cardstock (grain short)

LINERS FOR DRAWERS
three $1^{1}/_{4}$" × 6" (3.2cm × 15.2cm)
pieces of decorative paper
(grain short)

SLEEVE WRAPS
two $2^{1}/_{16}$" (5.2cm) decorative paper
squares

COVER FOR PYRAMID BOOK
$1^{3}/_{4}$" × $3^{1}/_{2}$" (4.4cm × 8.9cm) piece
of cardstock (grain short)

PAGES FOR PYRAMID BOOK
three $1^{5}/_{8}$" × $3^{1}/_{4}$" (4.1cm × 8.3cm)
pieces of text paper (grain short)

LARGE TOPPER
$2^{1}/_{4}$" (5.7cm) square piece of
cardstock

SMALL TOPPER
$1^{3}/_{4}$" (4.4cm) square piece of
cardstock

OPTIONAL
feet

> > THE MATCHBOX MARVEL is intended to spark your imagination and stimulate you to experiment. Matchboxes can be joined together and stacked in a huge variety of ways. The drawers can hold keepsakes, photos and tiny objects. Play with groups of 5, 9, 11 or more empty matchboxes, and combine and sketch different configurations. Decorate the matchboxes, then refer to your sketches and assemble them into finished Matchbox Marvels!

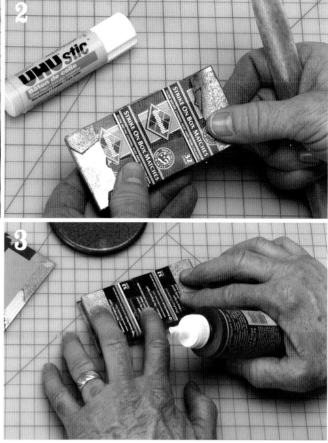

PATTERN FOR MATCHBOX MARVEL

Enlarge pattern at 118% to bring to full size.

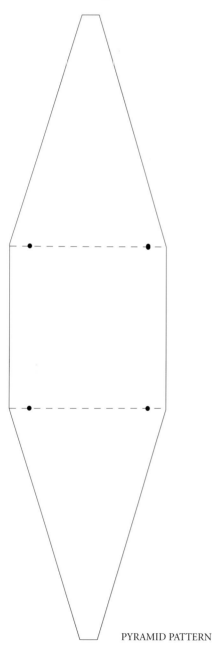

PYRAMID PATTERN

1 COVER MATBOARD AND MATCHBOXES

Cover the top and bottom matboards with the cover papers (for instructions, see pages 13–14). Run a glue stick over the back surface of one decorative drawer liner paper. Place one end of the liner at the midpoint of one drawer interior and wrap the liner tightly around the entire drawer and back to the inside. Burnish the liner to all the surfaces it touches on the drawer. Line the two remaining drawers in the same fashion.

2 MAKE SLEEVE UNIT

Insert the drawers back into the sleeves and line them up side by side. Place a short length of transparent tape across the length on the top and bottom of the sleeves to hold them together. Glue up the back surface of both sleeve wraps and attach them to the ends of the sleeve unit, as shown. Burnish wraps in place.

3 ATTACH BOARDS TO SLEEVE UNIT

Spread a thin coat of craft glue or PVA over the top surface of the sleeve unit. Turn the unit over and attach it to the inside surface of one covered board, centered on all sides, as shown. Turn the sleeve unit over and glue the second covered matboard to the top, in alignment with the bottom matboard. Place under a weight to dry.

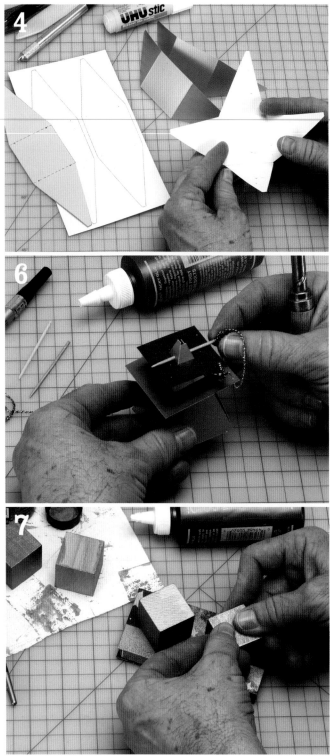

4 CUT AND GLUE PYRAMID COMPONENTS

Trace the pyramid pattern twice to the inside surface of the pyramid cardstock. Each time, pierce four holes through the dots on the pattern to indicate score lines. Cut out the pyramid sides and valley score each side twice, using the pierced holes for ruler alignment. Glue the pyramid sides together at right angles with the insides faceup, as shown. Burnish.

5 CREATE TOPPERS

Place the cardstock for each topper facedown on your work surface. Measure in $^5/_8$" (16mm) from the sides and draw a border on both toppers. Cut out the inner squares (for instructions, see page 49). Punch a $^1/_{16}$" (2mm) hole in the center of two opposite pyramid sides, $^1/_2$" (13mm) down from the tops.

6 ASSEMBLE PYRAMID

Dye a toothpick with a marker and tie a string around one end. Add a dab of white glue to secure the knot. Punch a $^1/_{16}$" (2mm) hole in one corner of the small topper and tie the toothpick to the hole, with 3" (7.6cm) of string between the toothpick and the corner. Place the toppers on the upright sides and run the toothpick through the holes to keep the pyramid closed.

7 ADD FEET

Paint or stain two wooden blocks. When the paint has dried, glue the blocks to the bottom of the structure to create feet. Place under a weight to dry.

TIP

When your handheld hole punch gets dull, punch ten or so holes in waxed paper to sharpen the punch.

8 MAKE AND INSERT BOOKS

Fold the page papers in half, then nestle them together to create a
12-page section. Valley score the book cover cardstock vertically
down the center and sew the section to the cover (for instructions,
see page 15). Place the book inside the pyramid. Make three tiny
books for the matchbox drawers, if desired.

9 MAKE ADDITIONAL COMPONENTS

Create additional components as desired. Here, I have glued one-
drawer and two-drawer units to the top of the three-drawer unit,
to create a pyramidal-shaped base. The pyramid structure can be
set on top or permanently glued in place.

ALTERNATE ENDINGS

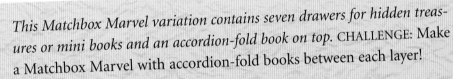

*This Matchbox Marvel variation contains seven drawers for hidden treas-
ures or mini books and an accordion-fold book on top.* CHALLENGE: Make
a Matchbox Marvel with accordion-fold books between each layer!

BOOK IN A BOX

TOOLS AND MATERIALS

basic tool kit (page 8)

BOOK BODY
7¹⁄₂" × 8¹⁄₂" (19.1cm × 21.6cm)
piece of decorative text paper
(grain short)

PAGES
nine 3¹⁄₄" × 3¹⁄₂" (8.3cm × 8.9cm)
pieces of text paper (grain short)

COVERS FOR PAGES
three 3¹⁄₄" × 3³⁄₄" (8.3cm × 9.5cm)
pieces of cardstock (grain short)

STIFFENERS
four 2" × 3¹⁄₂" (5.1cm × 8.9cm)
pieces of cardstock (grain long)

SPINE
3¹⁄₂" × 3³⁄₄" (8.9cm × 9.5cm) piece
of cardstock (grain short)

BOOK SLEEVE
3¹⁄₄" × 11" (8.3cm × 27.9cm) piece
of cardstock (grain short)

SEWING STATION TEMPLATE
3" × 3¹⁄₄" (7.6cm × 8.3cm) piece of
scrap cardstock (grain short)

OPTIONAL
box: 7³⁄₄" × 11" (19.7cm × 27.9cm)
piece of cardstock (grain short)

box sleeve: 2¹⁄₂" × 11" (6.4cm ×
27.9cm) piece of cardstock
(grain short)

small brass finding

> > THE BOOK IN A BOX RESULTED FROM A PERSONAL CHALLENGE to turn a piece of text paper into a structure to hold sewn sections. The sturdy book body is simple to make with just five folds. A removable cardstock spine hides two of the three sections and makes this miniature book delightfully interactive. Up to four books fit comfortably inside the accompanying box, or you can make a cardstock sleeve for each book.

1 FOLD BOOK BODY

Place the paper for the book body facedown in a vertical position. Measure from the left and draw light vertical pencil lines at 3½" (8.9cm) and 4" (10.2cm). Fold the right edge to the left line and crease. Open the fold. Fold the left edge to the right line and crease, then fold the right edge over to the left again, as shown.

2 FOLD AND MARK BOOK BODY

Fold the bottom edge to the top edge and crease. Fold the top edge down, flush with the bottom fold, then crease. Turn the book body over left to right. Fold the top edge to the bottom fold and crease. Draw an arrow near the bottom edge pointing to the right, as shown.

3 MAKE SECTIONS

Fold nine page papers in half with the folds parallel to the 3¼" (8.3cm) height. Crease each fold. Make three sections of three folios each. Score the sewing station cardstock down the center, parallel to the 3¼" (8.3cm) height. Make marks on the fold ½" (13mm), 1⅝" (4.1cm) and 2¾" (7.0cm) from the top edge.

4 PREPARE COVERS

Place three cardstock cover pieces facedown in a horizontal position. Measuring 1⅞" (4.8cm) from the left, draw a vertical pencil line down the center of each cover. Valley score each line, then fold and crease each score.

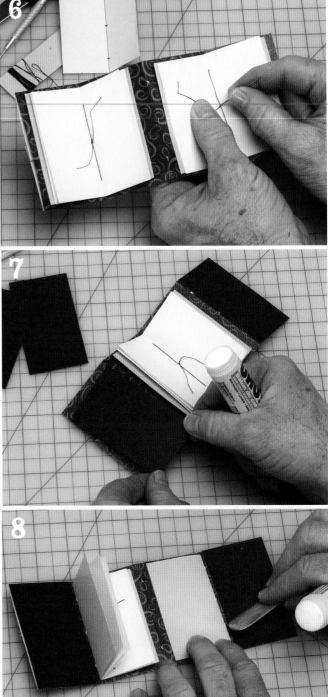

5 SEW SECTIONS TO COVERS

Place one cover, one section and the sewing template in the center valley fold of the book body, centered top to bottom, with the arrow on the right side pointing up. Pierce three holes. Remove the template and sew the cover/section unit in place, with the knot on the inside (for instructions, see page 15).

6 SEW IN REMAINING SECTIONS

Turn the book body over left to right. Pierce holes in the two remaining cover/sections and valley folds on the book body and sew in place.

7 ATTACH FIRST STIFFENERS

Place the book body horizontally with the arrow on the right side. Run a glue stick over the plain surface of one stiffener and attach to the right panel over the arrow, with the right edge of the stiffener flush with the right edge of the book body, and the tops and bottoms flush. Burnish. Attach stiffener to the left panel. Burnish.

8 ATTACH REMAINING STIFFENERS

Flip the book body over and attach the two remaining stiffeners to the left and right panels as described above. Burnish.

TIP The spine folds create a *capacity fold*, since they form a U-shape and are intended to have something inserted in the middle. It is easy to score folds that are close together if you score from left to right (or right to left, if you are left-handed) and allow your ruler to hold down completed scores as you move across the cardstock.

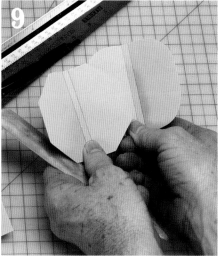

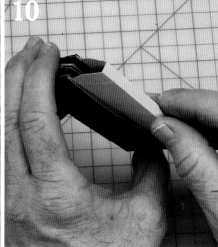

9 PREPARE SPINE

Place the spine cardstock facedown with the 3½" (8.9cm) height running vertically. Measuring from the left, draw vertical lines at 1¾" (4.4cm) and 2" (5.1cm). Valley score, fold and crease these lines. Trim the four corners as shown above—1" (2.5cm) down each side—or use a circle template to round each corner.

10 INSERT SPINE

Insert the spine into the openings between the stiffeners. If the spine is too tight, trim a sliver off the top. Gently push the spine all the way in. Embellish book covers and spine as desired.

11 MAKE SLEEVE AND BOX

Make a custom-fitted sleeve for your book (for instruction, see pages 17–18). If desired, place the book in a cardstock box (for instruction, see pages 20–21) with its own custom-fitted sleeve. Embellish the box and sleeves.

ALTERNATE ENDINGS

This Book in a Box variation features a plain cardstock box festooned with decorative paper and metal and bone beads. The sections in the book block are sewn into covers with throwouts, and the pockets contain tiny feathers.

SPECIMEN BOOK

TOOLS AND MATERIALS

basic tool kit (page 8)

black acrylic paint

paintbrush

BOTTOM AND LONG SIDES OF BOX
$3\frac{1}{4}$" × $3\frac{1}{2}$" (8.3cm × 8.9cm) piece of matboard (grain short)

DOORS AND SHORT SIDES OF BOX
$2\frac{1}{8}$" × $4\frac{7}{8}$" (5.4cm × 12.4cm) piece of matboard (grain long)

COVER PAPER FOR BOX
$3\frac{7}{8}$" × $5\frac{1}{8}$" (9.8cm × 13.0cm) piece of decorative paper (grain long)

COVER PAPER FOR DOORS
$2\frac{7}{8}$" × $4\frac{1}{8}$" (7.3cm × 10.5cm) piece of decorative paper (grain long)

WINDOW FRAME AND DOOR HINGES
$2\frac{1}{8}$" × 9" (5.4cm × 22.9cm) piece of cardstock (grain short)

WINDOW ON FRONT OF BOX
$2\frac{1}{8}$" × $3\frac{3}{8}$" (5.4cm × 8.6cm) piece of 4mm polyester film

BOOK COVER
$2\frac{1}{8}$" × $6\frac{1}{2}$" (5.4cm × 16.5cm) piece of cardstock (grain short)

PAGES
four $1\frac{7}{8}$" × $6\frac{1}{4}$" (4.8cm × 15.9cm) pieces of text paper (grain short)

> > MY DESIRE TO SHOWCASE AN ANCIENT SHARK'S TOOTH led to the creation of the Specimen Book. The tiny airtight and dustproof box has a crystal clear viewing window, doors to protect the window, and a book on the back to record the evolutionary history of sharks. This interactive structure can be made in any size and housed in a sleeve or box for further protection.

1 PREPARE BOX COMPONENTS

Place the matboard for the bottom and long sides of the box horizontally and draw light vertical pencil lines 2" (5.1cm) and 2¾" (7.0cm) from the left edge. Cut the matboard into three pieces on these lines. Place the matboard for the doors and short sides of the box horizontally and draw light vertical pencil lines 3⅜" (8.6cm) and 4⅛" (10.5cm) from the left edge. Cut the matboard into three pieces on these lines. Write "doors" lightly in pencil on the largest piece.

2 BEGIN CONSTRUCTING BOX

Apply craft glue or PVA to one long edge of the box bottom. Hold the box bottom down and attach one long side to the glued edge. Push against the bottom of the side with a piece of scrap matboard for 20 seconds. Attach the opposite side in a similar manner.

3 FINISH BOX

Stand the partially assembled box on end. Apply craft glue or PVA to the top three edges and attach one short side. Square up all the edges and push down on the short side for 20 seconds. Attach the second short side to the opposite end in a similar manner.

4 ADD DECORATIVE PAPER

Place the box cover paper facedown in a horizontal position. Draw a light horizontal pencil line ⅞" (22mm) from the top and a vertical pencil line ⅞" (22mm) from the left edge. Run a glue stick over the outside surface of the box bottom and attach it to the cover paper using the corner formed by the drawn lines for precise placement. Turn over and lightly burnish the cover paper to the box bottom.

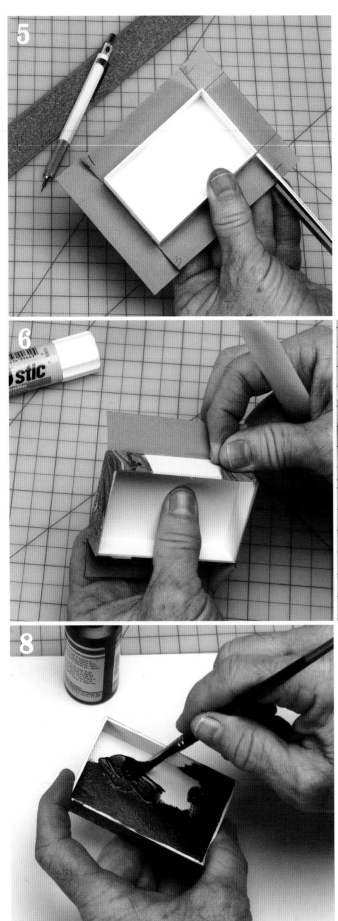

5 CUT SIDES

Place the edge of your ruler against the right side of the box. Draw light pencil lines from the corners of the box to the top and bottom edges of the cover paper. Use scissors to cut the lines numbered 1, 2, 3 and 4 in the photo, stopping at the corners of the box.

6 ADHERE TABS

Run a glue stick over the narrow strip of cover paper on the lefthand side and fold it up against the short side of the box. Then, fold the tabs tightly around the box corners and adhere to the long sides. Lightly burnish each section of the strip. Repeat with the narrow strip on the righthand side of the cover paper, as shown.

7 FINISH COVERING BOX AND TRIM PAPER

Glue up the two remaining strips of cover paper and fold them up onto the long sides of the box. Burnish lightly. Allow to dry, then trim the cover paper flush with the top edges of the box.

8 PAINT BOX INTERIOR

Paint the inside of the box with acrylic paint.
NOTE: *The interior of the box may be lined with paper as an alternative to painting.*

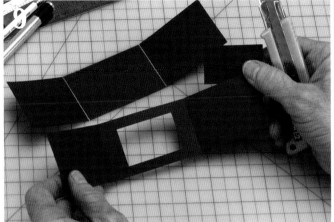

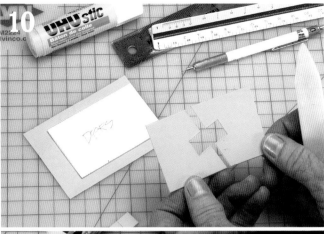

9 PREPARE WINDOW FRAME/ DOOR HINGE COMPONENT

Place cardstock for the window frame/door hinges faceup in a horizontal position. Measure over $2\frac{3}{4}$" (7.0cm) and $6\frac{1}{8}$" (15.6cm) from the left edge and valley score vertical lines. Fold and crease the scores. Open the cardstock and cut a window in the center, $\frac{3}{8}$" (10mm) from the top and bottom edges and $\frac{5}{8}$" (16mm) from the folds (for instructions, see page 49).

10 PREPARE DOORS

Cover (but do not line) the matboard for the doors with decorative paper (for instructions, see pages 13–14). Cut the matboard in half at any angle across the shorter dimension to create two doors. Cut a tiny window into the doors, as shown.

11 MAKE LEFT DOOR

Place the window frame/hinge cardstock in a horizontal position with the valley folds faceup. Run a glue stick over the back surface of the left door. Fold the left side of the window frame/hinge to the right and attach the left door to the hinge fold. Burnish. Open the door and trim cardstock flush with the edges of the door and window opening.

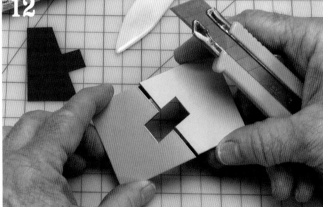

12 MAKE RIGHT DOOR

Fold the right side of the window frame/hinge cardstock to the left, then fold the left door over to the right. Run a glue stick over the back surface of the right door and attach it to the right hinge fold, with the cut edges of the doors touching. Burnish the door to the hinge fold and trim away excess cardstock.

13 GLUE IN SPECIMEN

Glue the specimen or artifact inside the box near the center and allow the glue to dry.

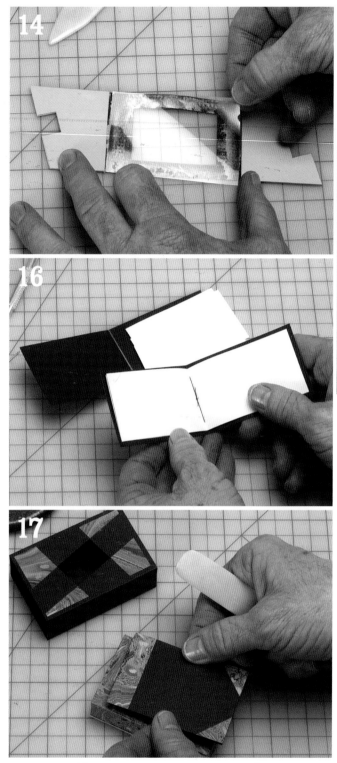

14 GLUE WINDOW TO FRAME

Attach the polyfilm window to the bottom of the window frame with glue or double-sided tape, being careful to keep glue or tape out of the window area. Place scrap paper over the window and lightly burnish the window to the frame.

15 ATTACH WINDOW/DOOR UNIT TO BOX

Apply a thin bead of craft glue or PVA to the four top edges of the box. Attach the window/door unit to the top of the box and carefully wipe away any excess glue. Place the box under a weight until the glue is dry.

16 MAKE BOOK

Place the book cover cardstock facedown in a horizontal position. Valley score, fold and crease vertically down the center. Fold the four page papers in half and place the folios inside each other to form a 12-page section. Sew the section to the inside of the book cover (for instructions, see page 15).

17 ATTACH BOOK AND MAKE SLEEVE

Decorate the front cover of the book as desired. Apply PVA to the outside surface of the back cover and adhere the book to the box, with the spine flush with the edge of the box. Place under a weight until glue dries. Construct a sleeve to keep the specimen book box closed (for instructions, see pages 17–18).

TIP Polyester film is available at most large art supply stores in single sheets or tablets. Polyfilm is more durable than acetate and is dimensionally stable in hot and cold environments. A 4mm or 5mm thickness is ideal for this project.

ADD SOME KICK!

Specimen Books are versatile! Divide your Specimen Book box into multiple compartments. Make larger boxes with artifacts, windows and doors on both sides, or replace the doors with a book glued to the top of the box, with a window cut in the back cover to expose the artifacts.

There are no doors on the top of the box pictured above. The diamond-shaped opening on the sleeve allows a tantalizing glimpse of the artifacts through the polyfilm window.

I divided the interior into two parts and painted one dark and one light to contrast nicely with the artifacts. The two sections behind the French doors allow one book to be devoted exclusively to each artifact. The book swings to the left so text can be read with the artifacts in full view.

ALTERNATE ENDINGS

Blue marbled paper on this Specimen Book suggests the ocean origin of the shark's tooth contained within the box. A pocket with capacity folds on the back of the sleeve holds a removable book.
CHALLENGE: Hinge three or more Specimen Books together, or mount a Specimen Box to a Matchbox Marvel-style base (see pages 80–83) with tiny books in each drawer.

THREE-SIDED TRIANGLE BOOK

TOOLS AND MATERIALS

basic tool kit (page 8)

eyelets or brads

patterns (page 99)

SIDES
8½" (21.6cm) cardstock square

LINERS
7½" × 8½" (19.1cm × 21.6cm) piece of decorative text paper or cardstock (grain short)

BASE*
4¼" × 7¾" (10.8cm × 19.7cm) piece of cardstock

BOOK COVERS*
3½" × 6" (8.9cm × 15.2cm) piece of cardstock

PAGES
2¾" × 10" (7.0cm × 25.4cm) piece of text paper (grain short)

HINGES
4" × 8½" (10.2cm × 21.6cm) piece of cardstock (grain short)

HINGE LINERS*
4" (10.2cm) decorative paper or cardstock square

TOPPERS*
4¼" × 7½" (10.8cm × 19.1cm) piece of cardstock

***NOTE:** The grain direction for the base, book covers, hinge liners and toppers is irrelevant.*

> > THE THREE-SIDED TRIANGLE BOOK came about as part of an ongoing series I started in 1995 to explore triangle structures as both vessel and book. The base, toppers and interior book are equilateral triangles and the sides are isosceles triangles. The triangular shape of each component is a strong and unifying design element. To date, I have made dozens of triangle book sculptures and feel I will be playing with triangles for life!

1 PREPARE SIDES

Place the cardstock for the sides facedown with the grain running vertically. Trace the side pattern three times, as shown above. Cut out the triangle-shaped sides.

2 PREPARE LINERS

Place paper for liners facedown in a horizontal position. Trace the liner pattern three times, then cut out the liners. Run a glue stick over the inside surface of one liner and attach it to the outside surface of one side, flush with the bottom and centered side to side. Burnish. Repeat with the two remaining liners and sides.

3 PREPARE HINGES

Place the hinge cardstock facedown in a vertical position. Trace the hinge pattern three times, and each time pierce holes through the two dots to indicate score lines. Cut out the hinges, then valley score the inside surface of each hinge, using the pierced holes for ruler alignment. Fold and crease each score.

4 ADD HINGE EMBELLISHMENT

Place the paper for the hinge liners facedown and trace the liner pattern three times onto the liner paper. Run a glue stick over the inside surface of one liner, fold one hinge at the score, and attach the liner to the hinge, just slightly above the fold. Burnish. Repeat with the two remaining hinges and liners.

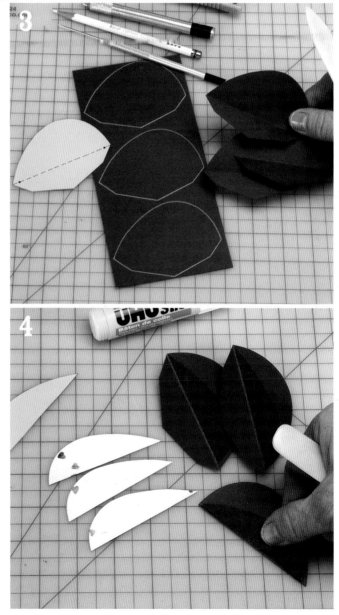

5 ATTACH HINGES TO SIDES

Run a glue stick over the large part of one hinge on the inside surface. Hold one triangle side with the liner facedown, and attach the bottom edge to the hinge, about $1/16$" (2mm) from the fold, centered side to side. Burnish the hinge in place. Repeat the gluing process with the two remaining sides and hinges, and turn sides over. Your sides, which will resemble those at the upper left corner of the photo, will be on the outside of the finished structure (see page 94). **NOTE:** *If you attach the sides to the hinges with the liners faceup, as I am demonstrating in the photo, the liners will be on the inside of the finished structure.*

6 PREPARE BASE

Place the base cardstock facedown and trace the base pattern onto the cardstock twice. Cut out each triangle base.

7 ADD HINGED SIDE

Glue up the inside surface of one hinge bottom and attach the inside surface of one base to the hinge, centered side to side, with the edge of the base about $1/16$" (2mm) from the hinge fold, as shown. Turn over and burnish the hinge bottom to the base.

8 FINISH ADDING HINGED SIDES

Repeat step 7 for the two remaining hinged sides so that all the sides are connected to the base. Turn the unit over and glue the second base to the first base over the bottom of the hinges as a liner/ stiffener. Burnish the second base in place.

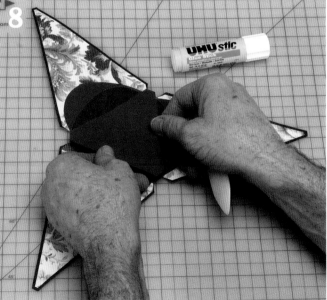

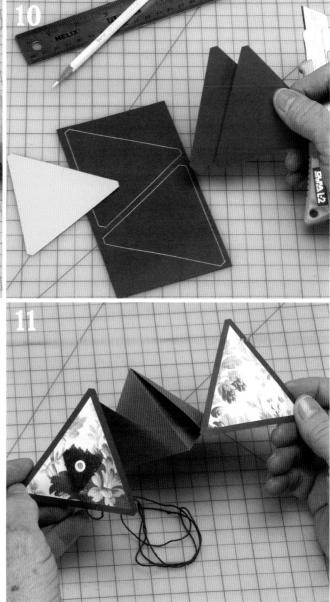

9 ADD TOPPERS

Trace the topper patterns to the inside surface of the topper cardstock. Cut out the toppers and place them on top of the upright triangle sides.

10 CREATE BOOK COVERS

Trace the book cover pattern twice to the book cover cardstock and cut out the covers.

11 ASSEMBLE BOOK

Cut out text-weight page paper and make the book, as described on pages 22–23. (The book in this photo was made with one page paper.) Line the covers and add a one-button tie to keep the book closed. Place the book inside the three-sided triangle structure.

ADD SOME KICK!

The rigid sides on this Three-Sided Triangle Book are made from matboard covered with decorative paper. Five loose pages with a painted matboard top cover with threads and beads hang from each side on wooden pegs. A triangle book fits inside and rests on pegs glued to the base.

12 ADD FEET AND EMBELLISHMENTS

Glue decorative paper strips to three glue stick caps and attach them to the bottom of the base as feet. Glue three more feet to the other side of the base and reassemble the structure with the insides on the outside, making your three-sided book reversible! Add any additional embellishments as desired.

ALTERNATE ENDINGS

Think of each Triangle Book as a three-dimensional canvas. Line and embellish the inside and outside surface of each side; attach tiny books or framed photos to the sides; make round or free-form toppers; or cut windows in the sides to reveal a ritual object inside this shrine-like structure.

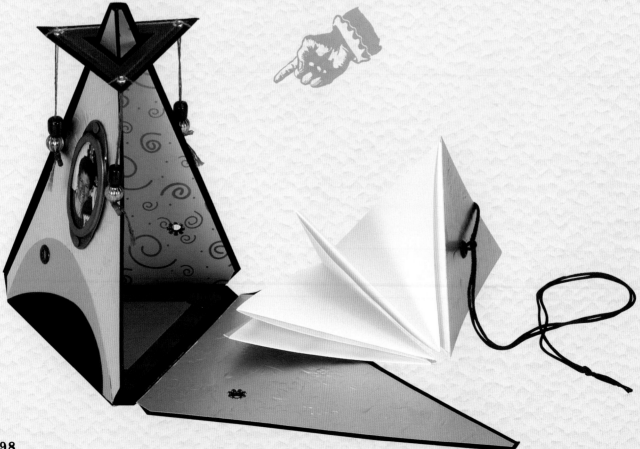

PATTERNS FOR THREE-SIDED TRIANGLE BOOK

Enlarge patterns at 200% to bring to full size.

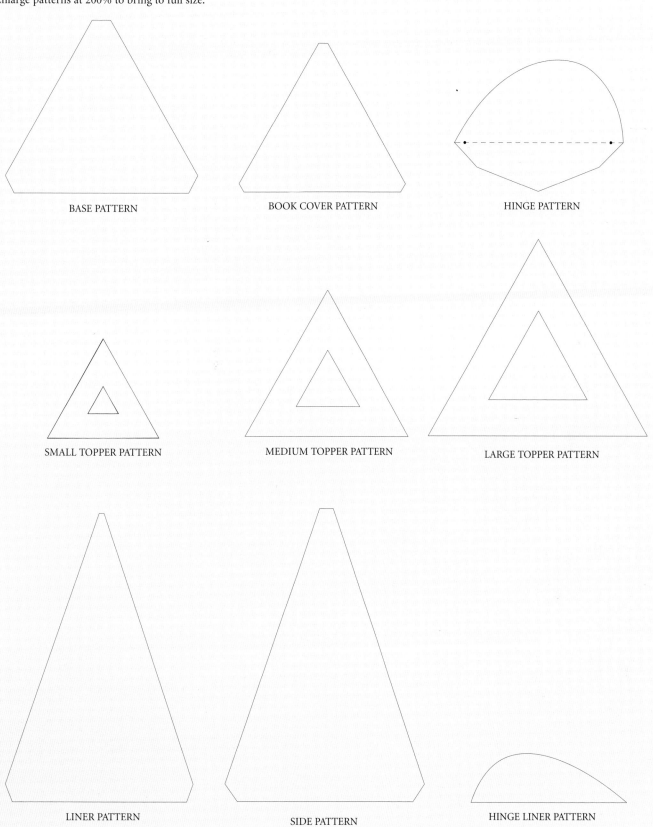

BASE PATTERN

BOOK COVER PATTERN

HINGE PATTERN

SMALL TOPPER PATTERN

MEDIUM TOPPER PATTERN

LARGE TOPPER PATTERN

LINER PATTERN

SIDE PATTERN

HINGE LINER PATTERN

FOUR-SIDED TRIANGLE BOOK

TOOLS AND MATERIALS

basic tool kit (page 8)

patterns (page 105)

hammer

BASE
5" (12.7cm) matboard square

COVER PAPER
6½" (16.5cm) decorative text paper square

LINER
4⅞" (12.4cm) decorative text paper or cardstock square

HINGES
8½" × 11" (21.6cm × 27.9cm) piece of cardstock (grain long)

SIDE A
two 8½" × 11" (21.6cm × 27.9cm) pieces of cardstock (grain short)

SIDE A PAGES
twelve 5" × 8½" (12.7cm × 21.6cm) pieces of text paper (grain long)

SIDE A SPINE WRAP
two 1½" × 8½" (3.8cm × 21.6cm) pieces of decorative paper (grain long)

SIDE A SHAWL
two 1½" × 11" (3.8cm × 27.9cm) pieces of decorative text paper (grain short)

SIDE B
two 8½" (21.6cm) cardstock squares

SIDE B SPINE WRAP
two 2¼" × 5¼" (5.7cm × 13.3cm) pieces of decorative paper (grain long)

SIDE B ACCORDION-FOLD INSERT
one 4¼" × 11" (10.8cm × 27.9cm) piece of text paper (grain short)

> > THE FOUR-SIDED TRIANGLE BOOK combines isosceles triangle sides with a square base to create a pyramid structure. Each side on this project stands on its own as a book. One or two sides can be lowered to create a shrine effect. Or, remove the toppers, lower the sides to a horizontal position, then turn this amazing interactive book sculpture over and reassemble it inside out! Build a detachable box with a drawer in it for a base, or hinge the sides of several bases together to create a pyramid village.

1 CREATE BASE AND HINGES

Cut ¼" (6mm) corners off the matboard base and liner. Cover the board, but do not line it (for instructions, see pages 13–14). Place the hinge cardstock horizontally, facedown, and trace the hinge pattern four times. Each time, pierce two holes through the dots before removing the pattern. Place the cut hinges faceup, then valley score each hinge using pierced holes to align the ruler. Fold and crease each score. Now make the sides, as described in steps 2–9.

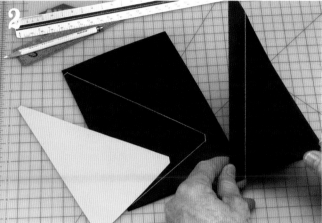

2 CUT AND SCORE CARDSTOCK FOR SIDE A

Place the cardstock for one side A facedown in a horizontal position. Measure over 5½" (14.0cm) from the left edge and valley score down the center. Fold and crease the score. Place the left edge of the side pattern on the fold, trace the pattern and cut out the side. Measure over ¾" (19mm) from the fold and draw a light pencil line. Open up the side and valley score, fold and crease the pencil line.

3 PREPARE BOOK BLOCK

Stack six side A page papers vertically and staple once at the center, close to the left edge. Hammer the staple lightly to flatten. Place the left edge of the side pattern on the left edge of the stack and trace the pattern. Cut through the page papers ¼" (6mm) to the inside of the right and bottom edges of the tracing. Shape foredges of pages if desired.

4 INSERT BOOK BLOCK

Open side A and place the book block snugly against center fold with equal borders on right side and bottom. Staple three times along the spine about ¼" (6mm) from the pencil line to bind the pages. Turn the side over and lightly hammer staples to flatten.

5 ADD SPINE WRAP AND SHAWL CLOSURE

Glue up the inside surface of one spine wrap. Starting at the pencil line, fold the wrap tightly around the stapled spine, burnish, then trim the wrap flush with the edges of side A. About halfway down side A, wrap the shawl paper around the angled sides, so one end overlaps the other in front. Crease the folds. Remove the shawl, trim the ends, then glue the ends together and burnish. Embellish as desired. Repeat steps 2–5 to create a second A side.

6 CUT AND SCORE CARDSTOCK

Place the cardstock for one side B facedown with the grain running horizontally. Trace side pattern twice. Cut out side pieces. Place one side piece faceup and draw a horizontal pencil line 1⅛" (2.9cm) up from the bottom. Valley score, fold and crease the line.

7 GLUE TOGETHER AND ADD SPINE WRAP

Run a glue stick over the inside surface of the bottom section and attach to the inside surface of the remaining side piece, with all edges flush. Burnish. Glue up and attach the side B spine wrap at the pencil line and fold tightly around the bottom to the back. Burnish, then trim the wrap flush with the side unit.

8 MAKE ACCORDION-FOLD INSERT

Fold text-weight paper to create an accordion-fold insert (for instruction, follow step 1 on page 21). Open side B and place the insert (with cut edges at the top) in desired position. Trim each side of the insert at an angle so it fits inside when side B is closed. Glue up the back panel of the insert and attach it to the inside back of side B, as shown. Decorate insert as desired.

9 ADD CLOSURE

Attach a button-tie closure to the top front of side B (for instructions on making button-tie closures, see page 23). Repeat steps 6–9 to create a second B side.

10 ATTACH HINGES TO A SIDES

Draw light pencil lines ⅛" (3mm) above and below the the valley fold on each hinge. Run a glue stick over the upper part of the hinge, using a glue guard to create a crisp edge at the top pencil line. Attach the back surface of one side A to the hinge, with the bottom of the side on the pencil line and hinge centered side to side. Burnish hinge to side. Repeat hinging process with the other side A.

11 ATTACH HINGES TO B SIDES

Attach the two remaining hinges to the B sides in a similar manner.

12 ATTACH FIRST SIDE TO BASE

Run a glue stick over the bottom part of one hinge, using a glue guard to create a crisp edge at the remaining pencil line. Holding the base with the unlined surface facedown, attach one edge of the base to the hinge at the pencil line, with the corners on the base in line with the corners at the bottom of the side. Turn the side over and burnish hinge to base.

13 ATTACH REMAINING SIDES AND LINE BASE

Attach the base to the remaining sides in a similar manner. Flip the unit over. Run a glue stick or PVA over the inside surface of the liner and attach to the base, lining the base and covering the small parts of the hinges. Burnish liner in place.

14 ADD TOPPER

Create one or more toppers with square or round holes in the middle to keep the sides upright.

Try Making Different Sides

The triangular sides are modular, and they can be hinged to each other in numerous ways. CHALLENGE: Hinge two or more sides at the base, or hinge two or more at the sides (accordion-style) or at the sides *and* the base. Experiment!

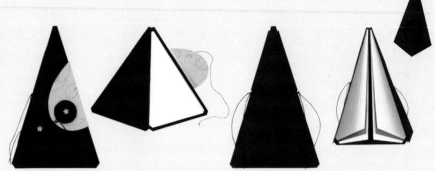

French doors, a modified shawl closure and shaped pages make the triangle side above a stately book structure unto itself. The closures are modified shawls with diamond-shaped windows.

The single hinge fold at the left on the triangle above also works well when placed on the right side or at the bottom. A wrap-around two-button tie and a section sewn inside the fold with the knot on the outside complete this side.

The foredges on the two sections inside the French doors on this triangle side meet at the center. Extend the foredges to opposite sides and intertwine the pages.

ALTERNATE ENDINGS

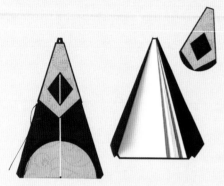

The three toppers on this Four-Sided Triangle Book are held in place with painted skewers. Collaged deodorant sticks serve as legs, and beads and dyed tufts of wool hang from one side.

CHALLENGE: Make a Four Under Cover (pages 64–66) with books in each corner, then add legs and mount your Four-Sided Triangle Book to the top surface.

PATTERNS FOR FOUR-SIDED TRIANGLE BOOK

Patterns are full size.

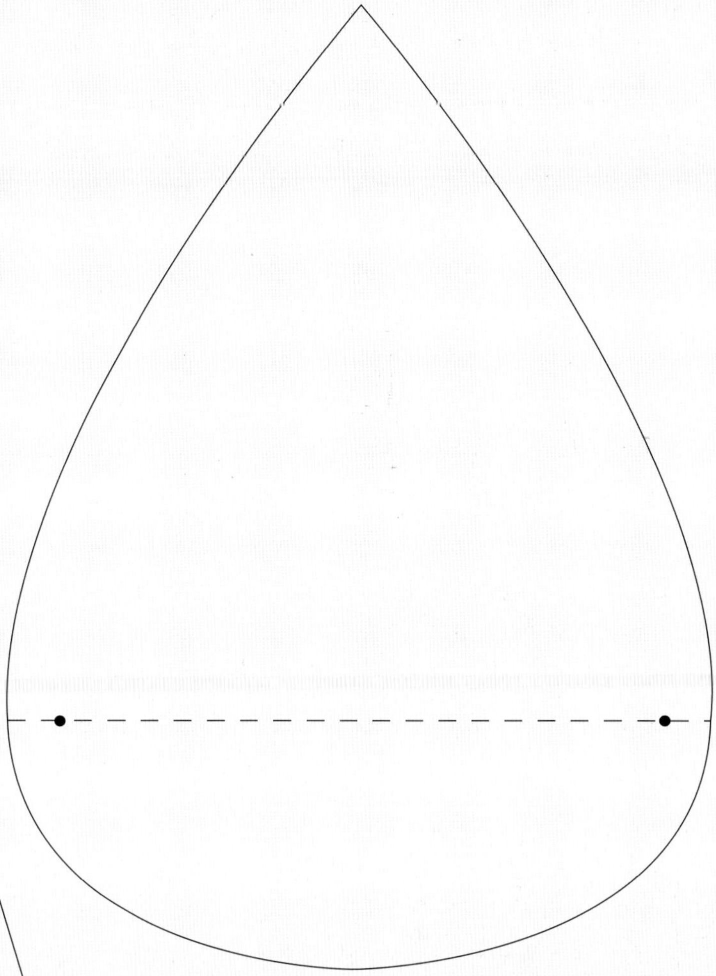

UNIVERSAL HINGE PATTTERN

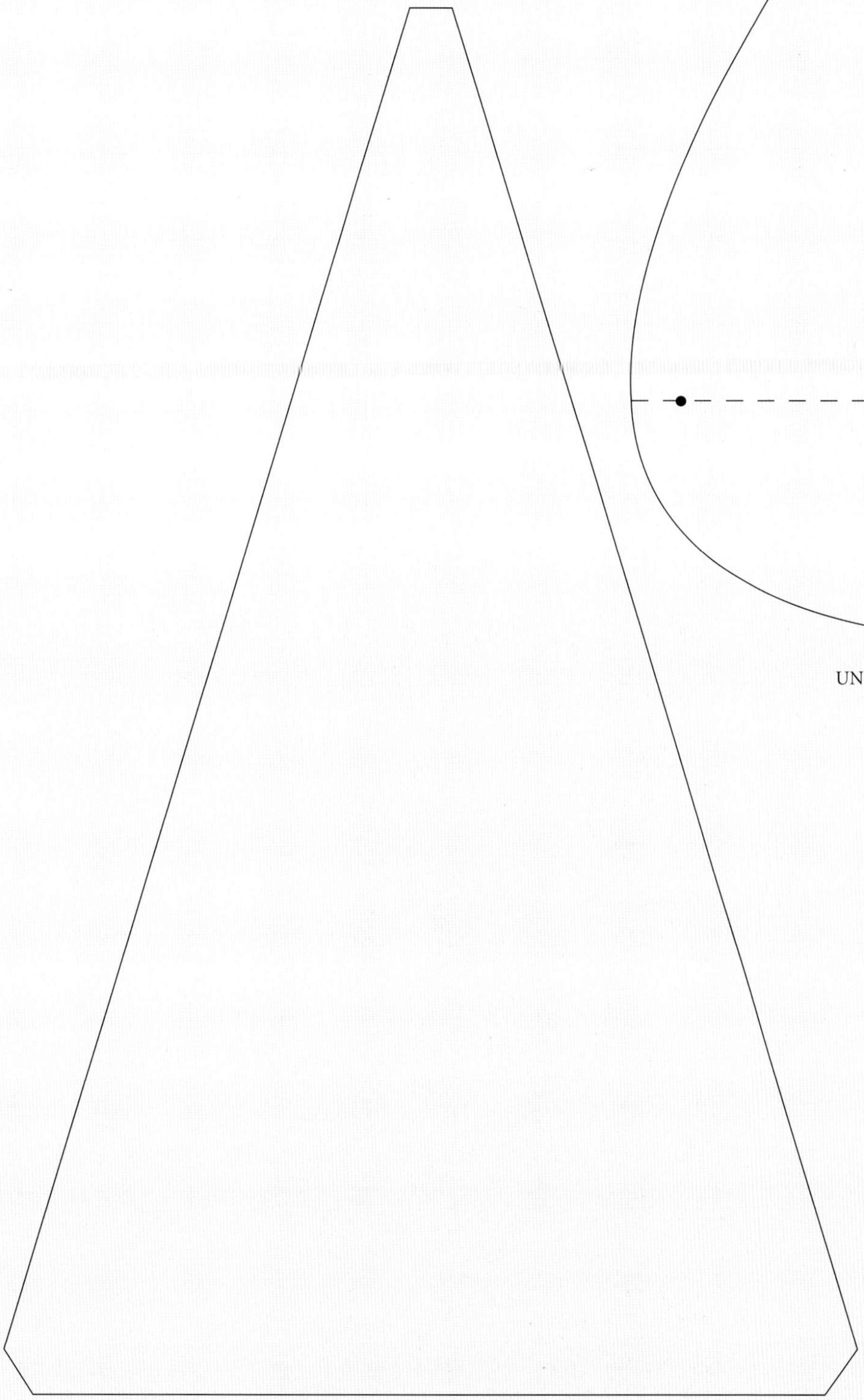

UNIVERSAL SIDE PATTERN

ARCHITECTURAL TOWERS

TOOLS AND MATERIALS

basic tool kit (page 8)

PORTFOLIO
7½" × 11" (19.1cm × 27.9cm) piece
of cardstock (grain short)

BOTTOM OF PORTFOLIO
4" × 5½" (10.2cm × 14.0cm) piece
of cardstock (grain short)

SLEEVES
four 5½" × 8½" (14.0cm × 21.6cm)
pieces of cardstock (grain short)

SLIDER GUIDES
four 2½" × 6" (6.4cm × 15.2cm)
pieces of cardstock (grain long)

SLIDERS
four 2⅜" × 6¼" (6.0cm × 15.9cm)
pieces of heavy cardstock
(grain long)

SLIDER STOPS
four ¾" × 2¾" (19mm × 7.0cm)
pieces of cardstock (grain long)

SLEEVE STOPS
four ¾" × 3⅝" (19mm × 9.2cm)
pieces of cardstock (grain long)

HINGES
four 3" × 5" (7.6cm × 12.7cm)
pieces of cardstock (grain long)

COVERS FOR SLIDER BOOKS
four 1¾" × 3" (4.4cm × 7.6cm)
pieces of decorative paper
(grain short)

PAGES FOR SLIDER BOOKS
four 1½" × 8½" (3.8cm × 21.6cm)
pieces of thin text paper
(grain short)

> > CONSTRUCTING UNIQUE BOOK SCULPTURES based on the Architectural Towers project opens up myriad design possibilities! There is no limit to the number, size and shapes of the towers, books and sleeves. Books can also be attached to the back of each tower, and you can cut windows in the sleeves to reveal letters or words on the book covers. When you are feeling particularly inventive, create an Architectural Towers variation based on Sagrada Familia, Antonio Gaudi's famous church in Barcelona, and send me digital images!

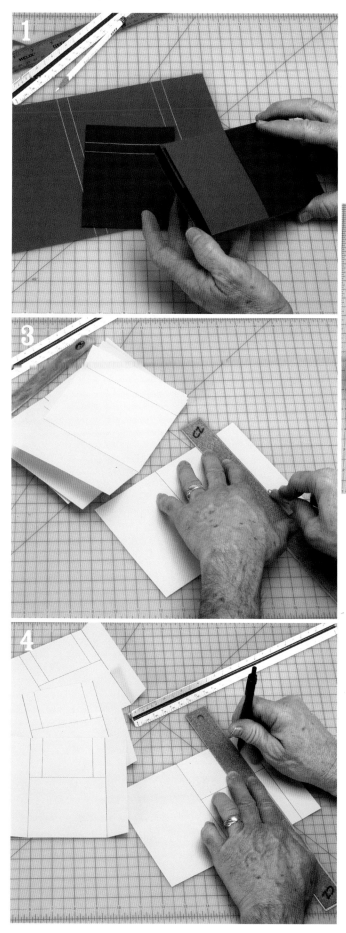

1 PREPARE PORTFOLIO

Place portfolio cardstock facedown in a horizontal position. Measuring from the left edge, draw light vertical pencil lines at 4" (10.2cm), 4½" (11.4cm), 8½" (21.6cm) and 9" (22.9cm). Valley score, fold and crease each line. Place the cardstock for the portfolio bottom facedown in vertical position. Measuring down from the top edge, draw horizontal pencil lines at 1" (2.5cm) and 1½" (3.8cm). Valley score, fold and crease each line. Erase all pencil lines.

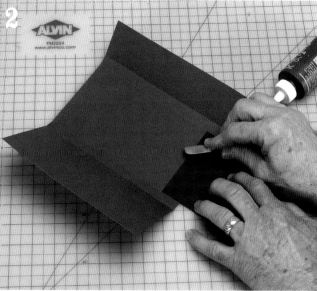

2 ATTACH BOTTOM TO TOP

Place the portfolio facedown in a horizontal position, with the smallest section facing right. Run PVA or craft glue over the outside surface of the 1" (2.5cm) glue flap on the portfolio bottom. Attach the flap to the bottom of the portfolio between the second and third valley scores with the valley fold on the portfolio bottom in line with the bottom edge of the portfolio. Burnish the glue flap in place.

3 SCORE SLEEVE CARDSTOCK

With one sleeve cardstock facedown in a horizontal position, measure from the left edge and draw vertical pencil lines at 3⅝" (9.2cm) and 7⅜" (18.7cm). Valley score, fold and crease these lines. Repeat with the three additional sleeve cardstock pieces. (There is no need to erase the pencil lines as they won't show.)

4 DRAW LINES ON SLEEVES

Place one sleeve facedown in a horizontal position with the narrow glue flap facing right. Draw a horizontal pencil line between the folds 2¼" (5.7cm) from the top edge. Draw two vertical pencil lines ⅝" (16mm) inside each fold, from the top edge to the horizontal line. Draw these lines on the three additional sleeves.

5 PREPARE SLIDER GUIDES

Place one slider guide facedown in a horizontal position. Measuring from the left edge, draw vertical pencil lines at $2\frac{1}{2}$" (6.4cm) and 5" (12.7cm). Valley score, fold and crease these lines. Repeat with the three remaining slider guides. Fold the narrow glue flap on one guide to the left and run a glue stick over the top surface of the flap. Fold the left section of the guide to the right, and burnish it to the glue flap, as shown. Repeat this process with the three remaining slider guides.

6 ATTACH SLIDER GUIDES TO SLEEVES

Draw a pencil line on each slider guide $\frac{1}{4}$" (6mm) from the top. Run a glue stick over the bottom portion of one guide, using a glue guard to keep glue out of the $\frac{1}{4}$" (6mm) area. Turn the guide over and attach it to a sleeve, with the bottom of the guide at the horizontal line and the left and right sides of the guide touching the vertical pencil lines. Burnish. Glue the three remaining guides to the sleeves in a similar manner.

7 ATTACH SLIDER AND SLEEVE STOPS

Glue and burnish the slider stops to the sliders with the bottom edges of the stops flush with the bottom edges of the sliders and $\frac{3}{16}$" (5mm) protruding from the left and right sides. (Stops can be glued to either side of the sliders; they will eventually be hidden.) Glue up either surface of the cardstock sleeve stops and attach them to the inside of the sleeves at the bottom, centered between the valley scores, as shown. Burnish.

8 TEST SLIDERS

With the back side up, push one slider through the bottom of one slider guide and pull until the stop hits the bottom of the guide. Test the slider by sliding it up and down in the guide. If the slider is tight and doesn't slide freely, remove it and trim a sliver off one side. Reinsert the slider into the guide and test again. Repeat this step with all the sliders.

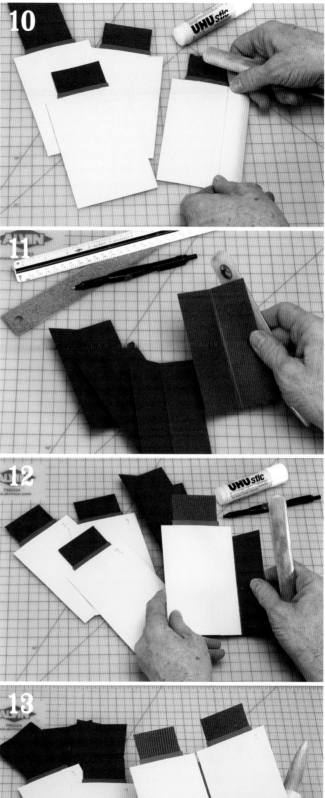

9 GLUE LEFT SECTION

Place one sleeve in a horizontal position with the slider pulled up and the narrow glue flap facing right. Run a glue stick or PVA over the upper 2" (5.1cm) of the left section and carefully over the sleeve stop at the bottom of the center section. Fold the left section to the right and burnish at the top and bottom. Repeat this gluing process with the three remaining sleeves.

10 GLUE RIGHT FLAP

Run a glue stick or PVA over the glue flap on the right side of one sleeve and fold it to the left. Burnish. Push the slider down until it hits the sleeve stop. Repeat the gluing process with the glue flaps on the three remaining slider/sleeve units.

11 PREPARE HINGES

Place each hinge cardstock facedown in a vertical position. Measuring from the left, draw pencil lines at $1\frac{7}{16}$" (3.7cm), $1\frac{1}{2}$" (3.8cm) and $1\frac{9}{16}$" (4.0cm) on each hinge. Valley score, fold and crease each hinge on the $1\frac{1}{2}$" (3.8cm) line.

12 ATTACH FIRST UNIT TO HINGE

Write numbers 1, 2, 3 and 4 lightly in pencil on the slider/sleeve units at the top of the glue flaps. Using glue guards, glue up the left side of one hinge to the pencil line. Attach unit 1 to the hinge with the right edge on the pencil line and flush at bottom. Burnish.

13 ATTACH SECOND UNIT TO HINGE

Attach the left edge of slider/sleeve unit 2 to the right half of the hinge in a similar manner. Burnish.

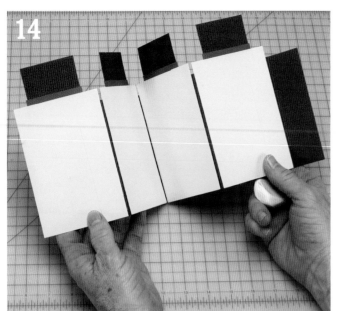

14 ATTACH REMAINING UNITS TO HINGES

Repeat the gluing process explained in steps 12–13, and hinge all four slider/sleeve units together. Glue up the left side of the fourth hinge and attach the right side of unit 4 to the hinge at the pencil line and flush at the bottom, as shown. Erase the numbers written in pencil.

15 FOLD SLEEVE UNIT

Fold up the sleeve unit so hinge 4 is at the top and facing left. Fold the hinge over to the right and place a glue guard in the fold.

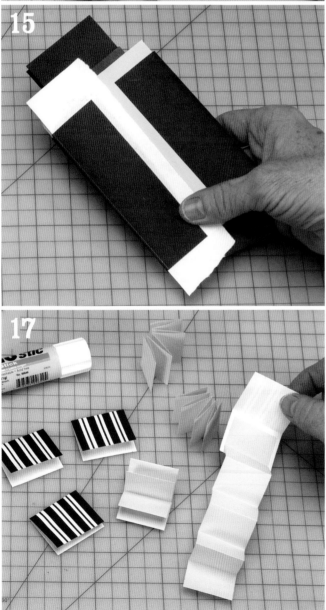

16 ATTACH HINGE TO PORTFOLIO

Run a glue stick over the hinge. Remove the glue guard and turn the unit over with the folded hinge facing right. Attach the hinge to the inside of the portfolio with the bottom of the unit slightly above the top fold in the bottom of the portfolio, and centered side-to-side between the two inner valley folds. Burnish the hinge to the portfolio.

17 CREATE ACCORDION BOOKS

Place the decorative text-weight papers for the slider book covers facedown in a vertical position. Fold each cover in half, top to bottom, and crease the folds. Accordion-fold the page papers (for instructions, see page 21). Glue the accordion-fold pages to the inside of the covers, as shown, centered on the bottom section. Burnish.

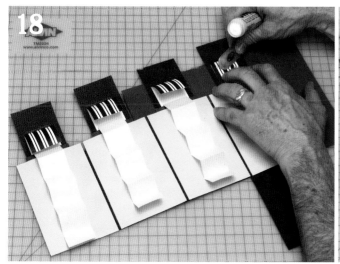

18 ATTACH BOOKS TO SLIDERS

Open the slider/sleeve unit and push the sliders all the way down. Draw a light pencil line across each slider at the top of the guides, then pull out the sliders. Glue the backs of the book covers to the sliders, between the top of the slider guide and the pencil line, and centered side to side. Burnish the covers in place, then erase the pencil lines.

19 EMBELLISH BOOK STRUCTURE

Close the pages and carefully lower the sliders, tucking the bottom edge of the covers into the slider guides. The books will be invisible when the sliders are down and come into view when the sliders are pulled up. Embellish as desired, and make a custom-fitted sleeve for the portfolio, as shown (for instructions, see pages 17–18).

ALTERNATE ENDINGS

Each sleeve on this variation project is a different height and width. The accordion-fold hinges allow greater extension when the structure is opened, and I've sewn sections with cardstock covers to the middle fold on each hinge.

CHALLENGE: Make an Architectural Towers variation with accordion-fold hinges, and sew in sections with stair-stepped pages similar to those in the Checkerboard Book (pages 36–41.)

WIRE-EDGE ALBUM

TOOLS AND MATERIALS

basic tool kit (page 8)

pattern (page 113)

three screw posts, $^3/_8$" (10mm) long

18- or 19-gauge wire

end cutters

FRONT COVER
6" × 7$^1/_2$" (15.2cm × 19.1cm) piece
of matboard (grain short)

SPINE
1$^1/_2$" × 6" (3.8cm × 15.2cm) piece
of matboard (grain long)

BACK COVER
6" × 9$^1/_8$" (15.2cm × 23.2cm) piece
of matboard (grain short)

FRONT COVER PAPER
7" × 8$^1/_2$" (17.8cm × 21.6cm) piece
of decorative paper (grain long)

FRONT COVER LINER PAPER
5$^3/_4$" × 7$^1/_4$" (14.6cm × 18.4cm)
piece of decorative paper
(grain short)

SPINE COVER PAPER
2$^1/_2$" × 7" (6.4cm × 17.8cm) piece
of decorative paper (grain long)

SPINE LINER PAPER
1$^1/_4$" × 5$^3/_4$" (3.2cm × 14.6cm) piece
of decorative paper (grain long)

BACK COVER PAPER
7" × 10$^1/_8$" (17.8cm × 25.7cm) piece
of decorative paper (grain short)

BACK COVER LINER PAPER
5$^3/_4$" × 8$^7/_8$" (14.6cm × 22.5cm)
piece of decorative paper
(grain short)

PAGES
twelve 5$^3/_4$" × 10$^1/_4$" (14.6cm ×
26.0cm) pieces of cardstock
(grain short)

SPACER UNDER FRONT COVER
1$^1/_4$" × 5$^1/_2$" (3.2cm × 14.0cm) piece
of matboard (grain long)

WIRE WRAPS
two 2$^1/_2$" × 5$^1/_2$" (6.4cm × 14.0cm)
pieces of decorative paper
(grain long)

> > I FAVOR NONTRADITIONAL APPROACHES TO BOOKMAKING, so it is no
surprise that wire-edge binding, developed by Massachusetts artist Daniel Kelm,
appeals to me big time. Stunning in its simplicity, it is also strong and versatile.
When Daniel lectured for the Washington Book Arts Guild in 2000, he brought
lots of book-like objects and amazing articulated sculptures hinged with wire-
edge bindings. My Wire-Edge Album employs this binding style in its simplest
form—a single hinge that smoothly rotates 180 degrees.

PATTERN FOR WIRE-EDGE ALBUM

Pattern is full size.

WIRE-EDGE BINDING PATTERN

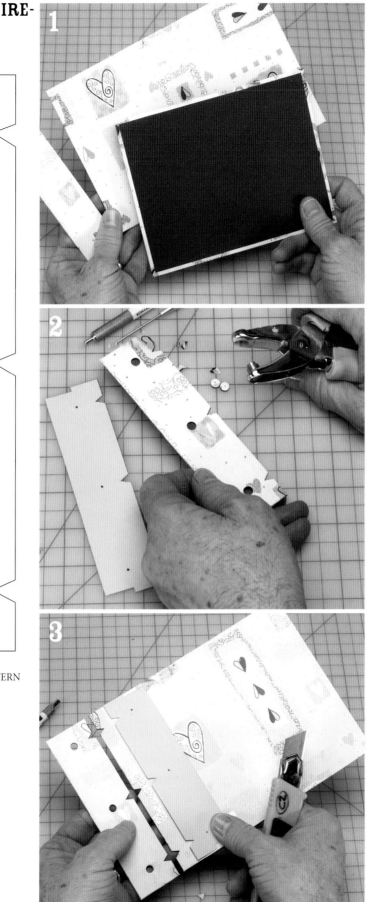

1 COVER MATBOARD

Cover and line the front and back covers and the spine (for instructions, see pages 13–14).

2 PIERCE SPINE

Position the spine vertically with the liner facedown. Place the spine pattern on top of the spine and trace the three notches onto the right side of the spine and pierce holes through the three dots. Remove the pattern. Cut out the notches, then punch three ¼" (6mm) holes, centered over the pierced holes (for accurate hole placement, see *Tips*, page 114).

3 TRACE NOTCHES TO COVER

Flip the pattern over left to right. Trace the three notches on the pattern to the left edge of the front cover. Cut out the notches. **NOTE:** *Flipping the pattern over ensures that the notches will line up precisely.*

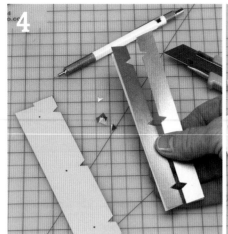

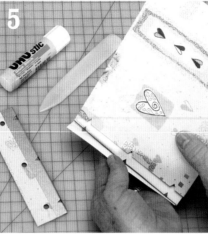

5 ATTACH WIRE TO COVER

Cut two pieces of 18- or 19-gauge wire 6" (15.2cm) long. Straighten the wires (see *Tips*, below). Glue up the inside surface of one wire wrap, close it partially to form a V-shape, then drop one wire into the fold and push the wire wrap firmly against the notched edge of the spine panel. Burnish on both sides. Attach the second wire wrap to the notched end of the cover in a similar manner, as shown.

4 NOTCH WIRE WRAPS

Fold the two wire wraps in half lengthwise and crease the folds. Place the wire wraps vertically with the folds facing each other. Trace the notches on the pattern to the fold on one wire wrap, flip the pattern over, and trace notches to the fold on the second wire wrap. Cut out all six notches.

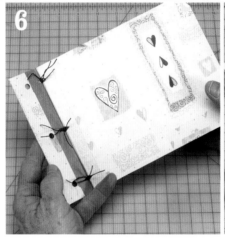

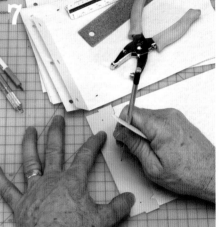

6 TIE COVER TO SPINE

Tie the cover to the spine at the notches with strong threads and embellish with additional threads, beads, etc.

7 PREPARE PAGES

Valley score, fold and crease one cardstock page 1¼" (3.2cm) from the left edge. Fold the narrow flap to the right. Place the straight edge of the pattern along the fold, as shown, and pierce holes through the three dots. Remove pattern and punch ¼" (6mm) holes centered over the three pierced holes. Repeat with the remaining pages (see *Tips*, below).

At a Cleveland workshop, Ohio artist Deborah Bachalder shared this great tip for straightening wire: First, straighten a length of wire with your fingertips. Then, place the wire on a cutting mat under a piece of matboard and roll it vigorously back and forth. In the image here, note the difference between the "unrolled" length of wire, at left, and the "rolled" wire, at right.

TIPS

For accurate hole placement every time, remove the hole catcher bar from your punch. Then, turn the punch upside down and center the hole on the punch over your pierced hole.

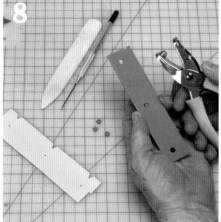

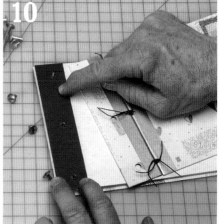

8 PREPARE SPACER

Place the straight edge of the pattern on the left edge of the spacer. Pierce three holes through the dots on the pattern. Remove the pattern and punch ¼" (6mm) holes centered over the three pierced holes.

9 PREPARE BACK COVER

Place the back cover in a horizontal position, with the liner faceup. Line up the straight edge of the pattern along the left edge of the cover. Pierce holes through the **three dots. Remove the pattern and punch** ¼" (6mm) holes centered over each pierced hole.

10 ASSEMBLE BOOK

Place the back cover in a horizontal position, with the liner faceup and holes at left. Slide the threaded bottom sections of the posts through the holes. Fold the flaps on each page to the right and place the holes in each page over the posts. Add the spacer, as shown, and the front cover. Screw the tops of the posts into the bottom sections and tighten.

ALTERNATE ENDINGS

The cover on this book sculpture features a wire-edge hinge and a polyfilm window in the door. The edging at the foredge and on the false spine matches the wire wraps and the borders on the covered mat-board base. I cut a hole in the matboard and glued an open-topped Specimen Box (pages 88–93) to the bottom. The legs are made from four empty deodorant sticks covered in paper and adorned with strings and beads.

SKY HOUSE BOOK

TOOLS AND MATERIALS

basic tool kit (page 8)

pattern (page 117)

16- or 18-gauge wire

round-nose and flat-nose pliers

end cutters

goggles

GABLES
two 4" × 4½" (10.2cm × 11.4cm)
pieces of cardstock (grain short)

ROOF
4" × 8" (10.2cm × 20.3cm) piece of
cardstock (grain short)

ROOF BOOK COVER
3½" × 7" (8.9cm × 17.8cm) piece of
cardstock (grain short)

PAGES FOR ROOF BOOK
four 3¼" × 6½" (8.3cm × 16.5cm)
pieces of text paper (grain short)

OPTIONAL
hammer and steel block

beads

threads

> > I HAVE ENTERED SKY HOUSE BOOK VARIATIONS in juried gallery shows and book exhibits, and it's exciting to me that the structure holds its own in both art and craft environments! The house, stilts and book components on this whimsical structure are detachable and fully collapsible. Additional books, text panels or objects can hang from the stilts, from the gables or from the bottom of the house. Think Las Vegas or Disneyland and design a totally original book sculpture on wire stilts with a roller coaster or futuristic ride on top! Is the sky really the limit with this project?!

1 PREPARE GABLES

Place the cardstock for one gable facedown, with the 4" (10.2cm) height running vertically. Measure 2¼" (5.7cm) from the left edge and draw a vertical pencil line down the center. Valley score, fold and crease the line. Place the angled edge of the gable pattern on the fold, trace the pattern, and pierce holes through the two dots. Repeat with the second gable. Remove the pattern and cut out both gables.

2 SCORE GABLES

Open one gable and valley score the inside surface on the two lines indicated by the pierced holes, then fold and crease scores. Repeat with the second gable.

PATTERN FOR SKY HOUSE BOOK

Pattern is full size.

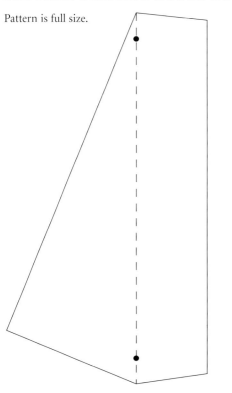

GABLE PATTERN

3 PREPARE ROOF

Place the roof cardstock facedown in a horizontal position. Draw a vertical pencil line 4" (10.2cm) from the left edge down the center. Valley score and crease the line. Place roof facedown in a vertical position and draw vertical pencil lines ¼" (6mm) and 3¾" (9.5cm) from the left edge.

4 FOLD AND GLUE GABLE

Place roof facedown in a vertical position, as shown. Then, fold one gable in half and place in a vertical position, with the angled fold facing left. Using glue guards, glue up the narrow panel on the right.

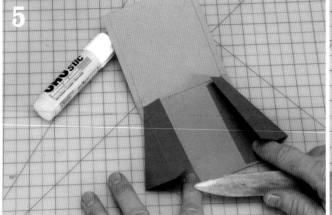

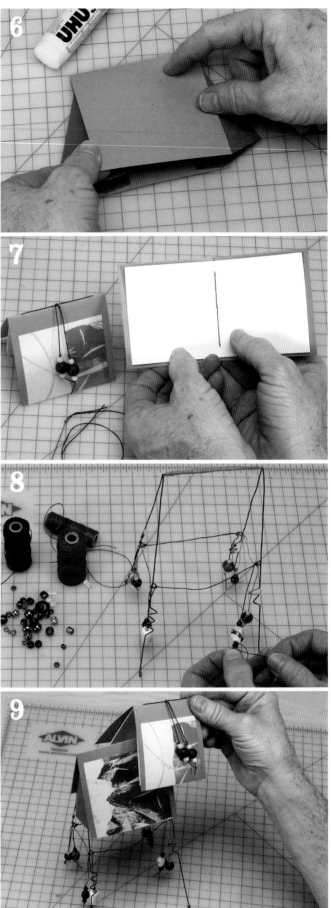

5 ATTACH GABLES TO ROOF

Remove glue guards, then turn the gable over left to right. Attach the gable to the bottom of the roof, on the right side, with the scores on the gable over the pencil line. Burnish the gable in place. Glue and burnish the second gable to the left side of the roof.

6 FINISH ROOF UNIT

Using glue guards, run a glue stick over the narrow panel on the top of each gable. Remove the glue guards and fold down the top of the roof. Burnish the roof to the gables.

7 CREATE BOOK

Place roof book cover cardstock facedown in a horizontal position. Valley score, fold and crease vertically down the center. Fold four page papers in half parallel to the grain, then crease. Place folios inside each other to create a 16-page section. Sew the section to the cover (for instructions, see page 15), with the knot on the outside. Leave enough thread to dangle beads, findings, etc.

8 CREATE STILTS

Wearing protective goggles, cut two 26" (66.0cm) lengths of 16- or 18-gauge wire. Straighten the wires with your fingertips. With your flat-nose pliers, make right angle bends 11⅜" (28.9cm) from both ends of each wire. Tie the top middle sections of the U-shaped wires together with thread. Shape stilts with flat-nose and round-nose pliers, and embellish as desired.

9 COMPLETE BOOK

With your round-nose pliers, bend small loops at the end of the stilts for strength, and adjust stilts if necessary for proper balance. Place the house and roof book on top of the stilts to complete your Sky House Book.

Working with Wire

Use flat-nose pliers (lower left) to make right angle bends and to grip wire while working, end nippers (far left) to cut wire, and round-nose pliers (upper right) to make circular bends and loops. You can work-harden and texture wire by hammering it gently over a steel block or anvil. Wire and bead book-marks (center) make excellent gifts and are a relaxing way to hone your wire-working skills.

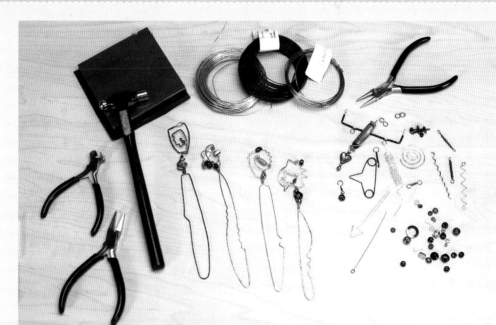

ALTERNATE ENDINGS

I attached a small book to each side of the roof on the house in this photo, and hung a larger book from one of the colorful skewers at the bottom of the house. I then tied beads and found bottle caps to the rusty wire stilts with waxed linen threads and glued pods made from chunks of corks to the bottom of the stilts to complete this Sky House Book variation.

STORYBOOK HOUSE

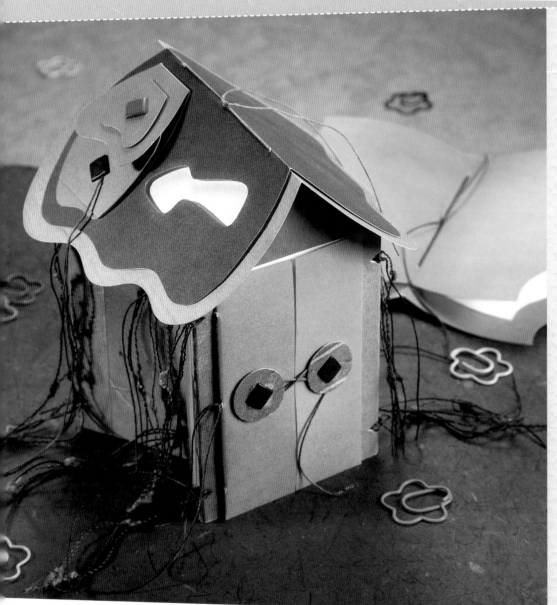

TOOLS AND MATERIALS

basic tool kit (page 8)

wire join pattern (page 125)

18- or 19-gauge wire

end cutters

silver metallic marker

FRONT PANEL
$3\frac{3}{4}" \times 6\frac{1}{4}"$ (9.5cm × 15.9cm) piece of matboard (grain long)

BACK PANEL
$5" \times 6\frac{3}{4}"$ (12.7cm × 17.1cm) piece of matboard (grain long)

SIDE PANELS
$4\frac{3}{4}" \times 8\frac{1}{4}"$ (12.1cm × 21.0cm) piece of matboard (grain short)

LINERS FOR FRONT AND BACK PANELS
two $7" \times 9\frac{1}{4}"$ (17.8cm × 23.5cm) pieces of decorative paper (grain short)

LINERS FOR SIDE PANELS
two $5\frac{1}{4}" \times 9\frac{1}{4}"$ (13.3cm × 23.5cm) pieces of decorative paper (grain short)

WIRE WRAPS
two $4\frac{3}{4}" \times 9"$ (12.1cm × 22.9cm) pieces of decorative paper (grain short)

SMALL BOOK COVER
$4\frac{3}{4}" \times 6"$ (12.1cm × 15.2cm) piece of cardstock (grain short)

PAGES FOR SMALL BOOK
three $4\frac{1}{2}" \times 5\frac{3}{4}"$ (11.4cm × 14.6cm) pieces of text paper (grain short)

LARGE BOOK COVER
$6\frac{1}{4}" \times 8\frac{1}{2}"$ (15.9cm × 21.6cm) piece of cardstock (grain short)

PAGES FOR LARGE BOOK
three $6" \times 8\frac{1}{4}"$ (15.2cm × 21.0cm) pieces of text paper (grain short)

ROOF
$6\frac{1}{4}" \times 8\frac{1}{2}"$ (15.9cm × 21.6cm) piece of cardstock (grain short)

>> SINCE WIRE-EDGE BINDING IS ONE OF MY ALL-TIME FAVORITES for three-dimensional book sculptures, I thoroughly enjoyed designing the Storybook House as the last project. The structure has six hinge joins made from wire, paper and thread, which allow the structure to collapse flat and to expand to a house-like shape—or countless other configurations! Two of the joins have a full 360 degree range of movement! Pages can be added at any of the joins, incorporated into a roof-book, or attached to the front or back of the structure.

1 MAKE FRONT AND BACK PANELS

Position matboard for the front panel in a vertical position. Draw a horizontal line 1½" (3.8cm) from the top edge. Measure over 1⅞" (4.8cm) from the left edge and make a pencil mark at the top center. Line up your ruler on the top mark and the ends of the horizontal line at each side and cut off the corners. Repeat this procedure with the matboard for the back panel, this time drawing a horizontal line 2" (5.1cm) from the top edge and a pencil mark at the top center 2½" (6.4cm) from the left edge. Dye all the edges with a marker.

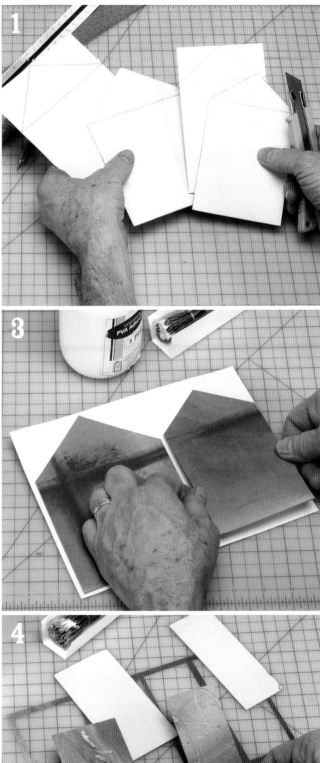

2 MAKE SIDE PANELS

Place matboard for the side panels horizontally. Measure over from the left edge and draw vertical lines at 2⅜" (6.0cm), 4¾" (12.1cm) and 6½" (16.5cm). Cut through the lines to create four small rectangles. Dye all the edges with a marker.

3 LINE FRONT AND BACK PANELS

Place one liner paper for the front and back panels facedown in a horizontal position. Glue up either side of the front and back panels and adhere them to the liner paper. Turn over and burnish liner paper to boards. Trim the liner paper flush to the edges of the panels. Use a second liner paper to line the other side of each panel, burnishing and trimming as before.

4 LINE SIDE PANELS

Line the side panels in the same manner you lined the front and back panels.

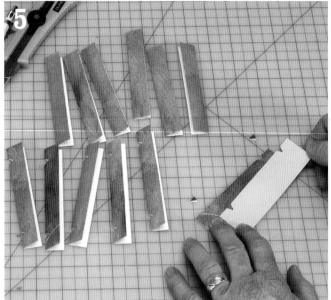

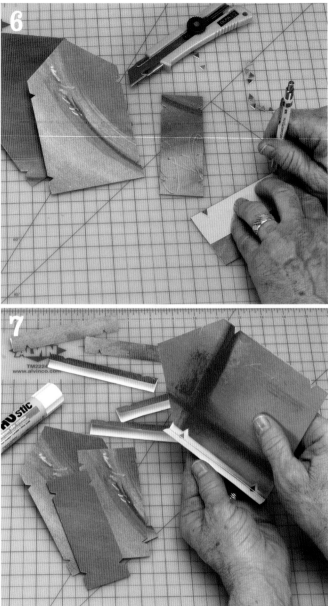

5 CREATE NOTCHED WIRE WRAPS

Place one wire wrap paper facedown in a horizontal position. Measure over from the left edge and draw vertical pencil lines at 1½" (3.8cm), 3" (7.6cm), 4½" (11.4cm), 6" (15.2cm) and 7½" (19.1cm). Repeat this process on the second wire wrap paper. Cut along each line and fold twelve wire wraps in half lengthwise, then crease all folds with a bone folder. Trace the two notches on the wire join pattern to the fold of each wire wrap, then cut out all the notches.

6 NOTCH FRONT AND BACK PANELS

Use the wire join pattern to trace notches on the sides of all the panels—front, back and sides. Cut out all the notches.

7 ADD WIRE AND GLUE WIRE WRAP TO PANELS

Cut and straighten twelve 4¹¹⁄₁₆" (11.9cm) pieces of 18- or 19-gauge copper wire (see *Tip*, below). Glue up the inside of one wire wrap and drop one wire into the fold. Push the wire wrap firmly against one notched edge on the back panel and burnish on both sides. Attach wire and wraps to all remaining notched edges on all the panels.

TIP

I drew a template on the top of a small matboard rectangle to quickly cut the twelve 18-gauge copper wires for the Storybook House project, then straightened each wire with the matboard (see *Tip* on page 114).

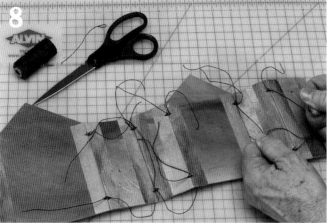

8 JOIN PANELS

Place the panels on your work surface, as shown. Tie the wires together at each pair of notches with strong thread. Decorate the panels if desired.

9 FORM HOUSE

Tie the outer two panels together at the notches. Tie on additional threads and embellishments if desired. Set the open-top, walled house structure aside.

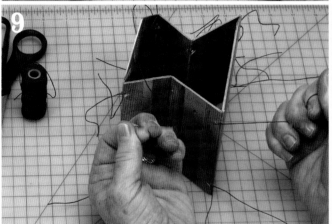

10 MAKE SMALL BOOK

Create a book to attach to the front of the smaller pointed panel. The rectangular book shown here has French doors and a two-button tie closure. I lined the inside of each door to hide the brads holding the buttons in place.

11 MAKE LARGE BOOK

Create a second book to attach to the front of the larger pointed panel. The book shown here has pointed covers and a wrap-around, one-button tie closure. I lined the inside of the front and back covers with the same decorative paper used to line the pointed panels.

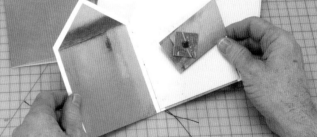

12 ATTACH BOOKS

Glue the back of the large book to the larger pointed panel and the back of the small book to the smaller pointed panel. Burnish the book covers to secure the books in place.

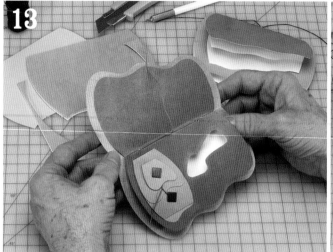

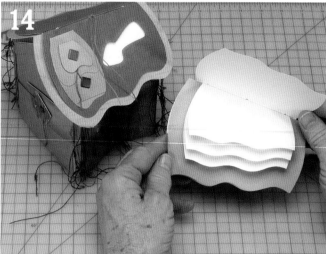

13 MAKE ROOF BOOK

Place roof cardstock facedown in a vertical position. Draw a horizontal line 4½" (11.4cm) from the top edge. Valley score, fold and crease the line. Shape the edges of the roof, and sew a section to the inside fold, or sew a book to the outside fold. Then, if desired, glue a tiny book to the top of the roof book, as shown, and cut a window in the roof to expose text on the first page.

14 PLACE ROOF

Place the roof book on top of the wire-edge house structure to complete your Storybook House, as shown at left. I created another roof book, at right, using the roof pattern on page 125 to give the book a different shape.

ALTERNATE ENDINGS

This Storybook House structure features lined matboard components and wire-edge hinges joined with jump rings. The roof panels bolt together to form a three-dimensional house with a door and floor (or deck, if you swing the bottom panel to the outside). The structure can be reassembled with the inside surfaces on the outside! When the bolts are removed, all the panels can be laid out on a flat plane. The accordion-fold book has matboard covers and fits inside the house structure.

PATTERNS FOR STORYBOOK HOUSE

Patterns are full size.

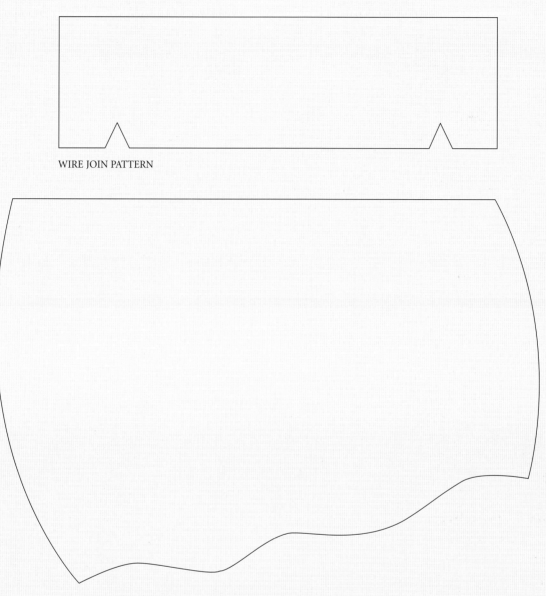

WIRE JOIN PATTERN

STORYBOOK HOUSE ROOF PATTERN (OPTIONAL)

RESOURCES

> > Below is a list of recommended bookmaking supply manufacturers, magazines and periodicals.
Check with your local retailer to purchase the tools and supplies used in this book.

Tools, Materials and Miscellaneous Supplies

Aiko's Art Materials Import, Inc.
www.aikosart.com
773-404-5600
art supplies and Japanese papers

Artistic Wire
www.artisticwire.com
630-530-7567
wire

Colophon Book Arts Supply
www.home.earthlink.net/~colophon
360-459-2940
papers, Japanese screw punch, tools, binding supplies

Creative Imaginations
www.cigift.com
714-500-1200 or 800-942-6487
extensive line of papers

The Creative Zone
www.thecreativezone.com
206-285-4136
book arts and papercraft workshops throughout the U.S., papercraft kits

Daniel Smith
www.danielsmith.com
800-426-6740
art supplies and papers

Dick Blick
www.dickblick.com
800-828-4548
art supplies and papers

Eckersley's Arts, Crafts and Imagination
www.eckersleys.com.au
phone for catalogue: 1-300-65-77-66
nine store locations in Australia

EUROTOOL, Inc.
www.eurotool.com
800-552-3131
tools

Fancifuls
www.fancifulsinc.com
607-849-6870
brass charms and findings

Fiskars, Inc.
www.fiskars.com
866-348-5661
scissors and paper cutters, circle cutters

Golden Artist Colors
www.goldenpaints.com
800-959-6543
acrylic paints and mediums

Hobby Crafts (head office)
1-202-596-100
retail craft stores throughout the U.K.

John Neal, Bookseller
www.johnnealbooks.com
336-272-6139
art and calligraphy supplies, papers, Japanese screw punch, tools and books

La Papeterie Saint-Armand
www.st-armand.com
514-931-8338
papermaking supplies and papers

NASCO Arts & Crafts
www.enasco.com
800-558-9595
art materials, tools, wire

New York Central Art Supply
www.nycentralart.com
800-950-6111
art supplies

Paper & Ink Arts
www.paperinkarts.com
800-736-7772
art and calligraphy supplies, papers, Japanese screw punch, tools and books

Pearl Paint
www.pearlpaint.com
800-451-7327
art and craft supplies, papers

Rio Grande
www.riogrande.com
800-545-6566
tools, wire

TSI, Inc.
www.tsijeweltools.com
800-426-9984
tools, wire, beads

Utrecht
www.utrecht.com
800-223-9132
art supplies

WigJig
www.wigjig.com
800-579-WIRE
jigs for making wire shapes, how-to online wire projects

Magazines and Periodicals

Book Arts Classified
www.bookarts.com
800-821-6604

Bound & Lettered
www.johnnealbooks.com
800-369-9598

dog eared magazine
www.dogearedmagazine.com

Expression Magazine
www.expressionartmagazine.com
858-605-0251

Rubberstampmadness
www.rsmadness.com
877-782-6762

Somerset Studio Magazine
www.somersetstudio.com
949-380-7318

Umbrella
www.colophon.com/journal
310-399-1146

INDEX

TRY YOUR HAND AT THESE OTHER FUN CRAFTS WITH GUIDANCE FROM NORTH LIGHT BOOKS!

Creative Correspondence
Michael and Judy Jacobs
You can create spectacular decorative mail! Inside, you'll find 20 project ideas, including letters and envelopes with photo inserts, stapled booklets and acetate address windows, plus clever self-mailers. With a basic how-to section, plus techniques for decorating and embellishing, you'll achieve great-looking results from start to finish.
ISBN 1-58180-317-6, paperback, 96 pages, #32277

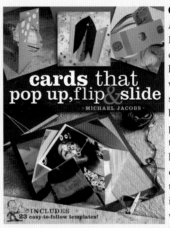

Cards that Pop Up, Flip and Slide
Michael Jacobs
In this creative guide to making dynamic, interactive cards, you'll learn how to craft one-of-a-kind greetings with moving parts such as pop-ups, sliders and flaps. Choose from 22 step-by-step projects that use a variety of papers—from handmade and printed to recycled—to create unique graphic looks. You'll also learn how to create coordinating envelopes to complete the look of your card. You'll be inspired to jazz up all of your cards with the fun and easy techniques in this book, including using inks, collage and colored pencils in fresh new ways.
ISBN 1-58180-596-9, paperback, 96 pages, #33109

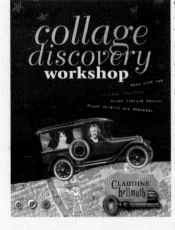

Collage Discovery Workshop
Claudine Hellmuth
This book is a medley of ideas, techniques and lessons on being an artist. Discover innovative techniques and demonstrations specifically designed to achieve the modern, eclectic collage effect that has become so popular today. Claudine Hellmuth will introduce you to the basics of collage, show you different image-transferring techniques and lead you through a series of creative exercises that are sure to ignite the creative spark in every crafter!
ISBN 1-58180-343-5, paperback, 128 pages, #32313

Altered Books Workshop
Bev Brazelton
A book isn't just a book anymore—it can have windows, doors, drawers and more. *Altered Books Workshop* gives you comprehensive instruction and inspiration for creating multi-dimensional art that is a reflection of your moods, thoughts and life. You'll learn how to turn old books into dazzling works of art by combining mixed media and papercrafting techniques with elements of collaging, journaling, rubber stamping and scrapbooking. You'll love learning the wide range of creative techniques for crafting unique, personalized altered books offered through the over 50 projects and ideas inside *Altered Books Workshop*.
ISBN 1-58180-535-7, paperback, 128 pages, #32889

These and other fine North Light books are available at your local art & craft retailer, bookstore or online supplier.